Setting the Gospel Free

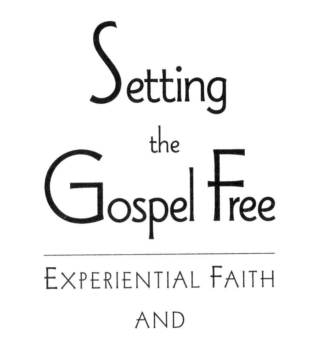

Setting the Gospel Free

EXPERIENTIAL FAITH
AND
CONTEMPLATIVE PRACTICE

Brian C. Taylor

CONTINUUM · NEW YORK

1996

The Continuum Publishing Company
370 Lexington Avenue
New York, NY 10017

Copyright © 1996 by Brian C. Taylor

Printed in the United States of America

Library of Congress Cataloging-in-Publication Data

Taylor, Brian C., 1951–
    Setting the gospel free : experiential faith and contemplative
practice / by Brian C. Taylor.
        p. cm.
    ISBN 0–8264–0938–5
    1. Spiritual life—Christianity. I. Title.
BV4501.2.T269 1996
248.4—dc20   96-8813
                                                     CIP

Contents

Acknowledgments

I offer my gratitude to those who made this book possible:

My wife Susanna and my sons Oliver and Sam, who teach me most of what I know and who always extend their loving support for what I am called to do;

The good people at St. Michael and All Angels Episcopal Church, who gave me the sabbatical during which this book was written, and who have, over the years, shaped my life by their nurture and challenge;

Lynn C. Franklin, my literary agent, who saw and believed in what I was trying to do, and then offered considerable editing insight;

Joko Beck, of the Zen Center of San Diego, who helped set the gospel free for me;

The Rt. Rev. Frederick Borsch, Bishop of Los Angeles, who gave me a very thoughtful and helpful critique of the manuscript;

The Rev. Samuel Hall, Dr. David Hackett, Bob Reid, and Dr. Marcia Landau, all of whom gave me vital encouragement along the way;

Eleanor Schick, who generously gave of her time and talent in doing the cover art.

Introduction

We live in a time of increasing interest in spiritual experience, and at the same time, decreasing interest in the Christian religious form. What is often overlooked in this cultural shift of attention is the depth of spiritual experience that traditional Christian religious form carries, with all its historical breadth and collective human wisdom. But tradition alone will not speak to people who are both justifiably skeptical of institutions and increasingly confident of their own authentic spirituality. For those who have discovered that an integrated spirituality has to do with such realities as relationships, work, and everyday consciousness, Christian tradition must be seen to be a vital reality that can actually transform its followers. The gospel must be set free into life: the only place where God is to be found.

The kind of Christian faith that is needed for our time is one that is *experiential*: using the Christian symbols and teachings in order to point to the truth in universal, real-life human experience. The kind of Christian practice that is needed is *contemplative*: using meditative prayer, liturgy, study, service, and other traditions in order to awaken to the immanence of God in the moment. In this book I therefore attempt to use the Christian form in an experiential, contemplative way, in order that its teachings may again come alive in our day.

This book is written primarily for the borderline Christian. On one side of Christianity's border are many who are hovering just outside and looking in. On the other side are those who are just barely within and looking out. These people on both sides of the border are those who are attracted to the richness of Christian tradition: its myth, ritual, community, and the person and message of Jesus. But they are also cautious about an otherworldly pietism or a dogmatic narrow-mindedness that in either case seems to exclude their own authentic spiritual experience that they know to be very real. What they often desire is a Christian faith that is experiential and opened out toward life; a religion that recognizes its truths can be found in other forms; a church that uses its theology and rites in a way that points to what is universal in the human experience of the sacred.

Many of us borderline Christians grew up going to churches that resembled a social club. We dressed up, behaved quietly, and interacted superficially. We didn't talk about prayer, pressing social issues, or our own personal pain and struggle. Because the church didn't look outward onto life, it spent its time looking inward, leaning on the insiders' symbols, music, and language of faith. The church provided an alternate reality into which believers could escape for a kind of brief vacation for the soul. This wasn't all bad, but in this sense the church functioned like a friendly, harmless cult. For cults don't focus out toward life; they focus inward upon their own private world.

My tradition heightened this cultlike atmosphere by using Elizabethan language in worship, which often made me feel as if I were in a very different and holy place. We heard words like *salvation*, *belief*, and *grace* without knowing quite what was meant by them: but somehow they vaguely assured us. We worshiped God singularly, like solitary planets circling the sun, each in our own orbital pattern. Youth groups, committees, guilds, and potlucks were offered as a way of getting church things done and being together socially. Our lives went on as they do, and church was offered as a kind of religious ornament. Even though the ritual and the community might have suggested depth and comfort, we were bored by its lukewarm piety and remained unchanged.

Others of us grew up going to churches that were centered around shame and fear. The promise of heaven and the threat of hell were held before us, and our eternal outcome depended upon whether or not we adhered to the church's way. Here we heard that our humanity was evil or untrustworthy. God was a stern judge who disapproved of us for being who we were. These kinds of churches also functioned as a kind of cult, but in a different way. Here there were very clear boundaries, inside of which one was expected to remain under the threat of dire consequence. Our behavior was expected to fall within strict limits. Conceiving of God differently or seeking God through other means was unthinkable, and so when we began to search seriously or behave unacceptably, we were in one way or another rejected. The rejection was total: we were not only unacceptable to the community, but unacceptable to God.

When the church put us to sleep or declared us unacceptable, we were disappointed and hurt, and many of us left. But we kept on seeking. We sought and found, to some measure, a more vital holiness through relationships, therapy, artistic discipline, suffering, traveling, recovery groups, and other religious traditions. We wondered why the things we discovered weren't taught to us in church.

Still others of us have remained in church all along but have been longing for more depth. We sense that it won't work to simply try harder or attend an uplifting weekend conference. We go through the motions, knowing there is more that is available to us in the Christian tradition than we are getting. But we also are near the border, and if it weren't for a few significant factors, we'd probably leave.

But whether driven out by boredom or abuse, or having stuck it out even though remaining somewhat unfulfilled, many of us are still haunted by the mystery of God and the clarity of Jesus. We long to surrender. We find something unspeakably tender and beautiful about being a part of the human community engaged in liturgical worship. We feel a call to belong to something that takes us beyond ourselves, something that exists in order to serve this broken world. We are attracted by the richness of the church's historical witness: selfless and joyful servants like St. Francis; contemplatives such as Thomas Merton; various broad-minded intellectual Jesuits; T. S. Eliot and other transcendent poets; and courageous social prophets like Martin Luther King. Like gravity, the pull of the Christian tradition draws us back, however reluctantly, at least to its border.

For those who are seeking something more life-giving than the boredom or abuse of their childhood religion, for those who want a deeper, more vital faith within the church, a different kind of Christianity must be explored: a more experiential and mature expression of God, prayer, Jesus, faith, conversion of life, and healing for the world. A Christianity must be found that is secure enough, big enough to honor the richness, diversity, and sacredness of all. We need to practice a religion that is specific in its mythic expression but universal in what it accomplishes. And for those who have come to know God as the source of all being through meditative practice, a contemplative approach to prayer will help the often limited religious concept of God to actually come alive.

However, it is not as if the church can simply provide this wonderful product for the passive enjoyment of the seeker. The seeker herself will need to struggle to find a way of making the Christian path, beneath its cultural and familial limitations, her own. She must work hard to use the depth and beauty of Christian tradition well; she will have to dig into the symbols, stories, and teachings of the church so that they will be able to carry, challenge, and change her life, so that they will inform, and reveal the sacredness of, her moments and days. She will also use whatever other life-giving disciplines and wisdom she encounters elsewhere as an integral part of her faith journey. And she must understand and overcome for herself the limited vision of the Christian church when it functions in a narrow and self-serving way.

The seeker and the church must break Christianity open into life, where Jesus intended our faith experience to be; this is the effort required. This breaking open sets the gospel free from its imaginary ownership and limitation by the church, and takes on the responsibility of moving it into our experience of God-in-life.

My motivation in this book is not to bring borderline Christians into the unquestioning "orthodox" center of the church. Being on the borders of religion is not such a bad place to be. As Jesus did, one can both be fully immersed in it and yet live on its edges. For one who is an Episcopal priest, leading a congregation into the traditions of the Christian institution, I for one must remain in this borderline place in order to keep sane and spiritually alive. Perhaps it is a question of being in the church but not of it. And while this paradox may have its discomforts, it also has its rewards. Here we learn to use the religious tradition respectfully but lightly, in a way that pushes us out of the church and back into the richness of our humanity. This book explores the challenge of living in this borderline place, a place of both roots and freedom.

The chapters that follow, then, will explore the abuse and use of religion, how our image of and relationship with God can mature and expand, where the following of Jesus' path may lead us in life, and finally how we can see God infusing all.

1

Religion Is Just a Form

I tell you, something greater than the temple is here.
— Jesus (Matt. 12:6)

LOSING MY RELIGION

One morning in 1991, I was sitting outside on my patio doing my habitual daily prayer and meditation. The sky was the deep blue of the high desert in early summer. It was my day off from work as an Episcopal parish priest; the kids were in school and my wife was out. It was the perfect time and place for an untroubled time of centering.

For some reason I still don't understand, a deep feeling of weariness came over my spirit. I had a tremendous, inexplicable urge to drop it all. I was weary of my tidy practice of prayer, my sense of "having" a spiritual life, my images and assumptions about God, Jesus, the priesthood, and the church. Somehow all of this had become a *thing*, a big important heavy thing which I was obliged to keep alive. I was tired of carrying this thing around. I allowed myself to taste the thrilling desire not to be religious. All at once I knew I wanted, for at least a while, to concern myself with just being human. Looking up at the sky, feeding the dog, attending to my children, cooking dinner . . .

suddenly it seemed so free and simple, unburdened by this religious thing I had created on top of my life.

Looking back on it, I can see that it was burnout that led up to this mysterious urge. In only a few months' time I had gone through an arsonist's devastating fire at the church, a messy public breakdown of a relationship with a staff member in which I became the villain, the beginning of an ambitious building program in the parish, and turning forty. Something had to give, and I was fortunate enough for that something to be a central factor for me: my religion.

On that fine summer morning I decided to give in to the urge. I didn't have much choice, really. My alienation from the church, always lurking quietly in the background, now had me by the throat. I didn't even comprehend fully what I was doing, but without effort or understanding I truly dropped something very big and important right then and there (just for the summer, I told myself). It fell away like an old dead skin.

The effect was immediate. I was scared deep down, but I was also free. What an exhilarating feeling, to just be a person, to let the moment be what it was without an extra layer of meaning. Work in the parish became, to say the least, a little strange, but fortunately my month-long vacation was coming up soon. During that time I fell back into an old interest in Zen, reading Joko Beck's *Everyday Zen* and meditating. That felt natural and real, and I happily passed the month as a mindful agnostic. However, I had no way of being prepared for what was to ensue upon my return to parish ministry in the fall.

Back in the round of liturgy, preaching, teaching, administering, and serving as pastor to people who came to me (surprise!) with their alienation from religion, I felt hopelessly trapped and empty. I was supposed to have something meaningful to say, and I had nothing. And yet like a coin-operated robot, I had to keep going anyway. It was horrible. I heard the words of sermons and liturgical prayers come out of my mouth as if they were nonsense syllables spoken by a "Star Trek" alien. Even worse, the whole religious enterprise seemed like a sham, a clever illusion created by fearful and grasping minds. We were all very busy greasing the cogs of a vast machine the purpose of which we had long ago forgotten. I couldn't even pray for help, for my prayers had lost meaning. I contemplated what else I could do to support my family and home. Nothing came to mind, and I knew that this was no time to make a big change.

I entered what was to be a year of therapy. Calling upon friends whom I could trust, I admitted my state of being utterly lost. They were sympathetic, but they couldn't help. I made my first *sesshin* (intensive meditation retreat) shortly afterwards at the Zen Center of San Diego. I began to feel some hope, not for my religion, but for my life.

Over the next year, a number of things slowly worked on me, transforming the emptiness into something spacious and powerful. Through therapy I brought my frozen fears into the light, and they began to lose their strength. By the grace of God, I was given at this very time a difficult relationship with my bishop, a perfect opportunity for working out issues of autonomous religious authority and identity. Meditation began to bear fruit, and I relaxed in what I could begin to call the holiness of God's energy within and around me. Strangely, I was drawn like a magnet back into one of my least favorite subjects of study in seminary, Christology (the theology of who Christ was and is). I found myself doing some hard theological thinking in a way that was more honest than ever before. I began to discover what I really thought.

Slowly the raw edge of religious alienation softened. Starting from zero, Jesus and God could begin to make sense in a new and refreshing way. Free of the burden of religion as a thing to carry, I could walk the Christian path lightly. Free to be honest, I could be myself and yet stand within the vast tent of the church's tradition. The specifics of it all didn't matter so much anymore. What mattered was the big picture: reverence, divine presence, redemptive suffering, the mysterious universal movement toward wholeness, our self-offering and patient practice. What mattered was life. I had lost my religion and gained faith. The gospel had been set free for me by being broken open into life.

One of the most helpful moments during this crisis was an offhand comment of Joko Beck's during a telephone conversation. I can't remember the context, but the words leapt out and burned themselves in my memory. She said "Well, you know, religion is just a form." I felt as if I had been beating my head against the koan of religion for over a year, and in this moment it all became clear. All of religion—its language, ritual, theology, and practice—is a form that can only point imperfectly to what is formless and perfect. When I heard Joko's words that day, something inside me let go. I was given the grace to rest in a simple, grateful awareness of God-in-life as I follow the Jesus way. That was enough.

JESUS SETS RELIGION FREE

I am fully aware that it is a risky business for religious leaders to live and teach this way. Nearly two thousand years ago, Jesus of Nazareth liberated his followers and got himself killed partly because he believed and taught that Judaism was just a form. Jesus knew that religion was not real, at least in terms of being some kind of permanent objectifiable thing. He taught that it was an imperfect and relative vehicle which, at its best, could only serve as a vehicle for what is real: the immediate presence of God. The reason the religious authorities were threatened was because even though Jesus practiced religion faithfully, he did not ultimately believe in religion. He believed in God-in-life. He knew that when religion becomes a Big Important Thing one must carry around, it replaces experience, and dies. When form, with its own dictates about correcting thought and conduct, becomes the most important thing, then religion begins to function as an idolatrous cult. It becomes a closed system, faced inward upon itself. It forgets about life and remembers only its own internal and imaginary world. Ironically and tragically, it actually gets in the way of what it is supposed to mediate.

Jesus set religion free for himself and his followers. He broke Judaism open into life. Jesus' gospel, his good news, was the proclamation of the end of religion as cult and the beginning of God-in-life. He brought the end of religion that required, through institutional power and ideology, a certain code of behavior, worship, and belief. It was the end of religion as a closed system. This death of religion gave way to a refreshing and liberating spiritual rebirth. Jesus shifted his disciple's gaze from the interior concerns of religious cult to the immediacy of God in each moment. They looked to nature, human celebrations, inclusion of the marginalized, relationships of love and forgiveness, the creature's very real union with the Creator, and the purpose of suffering. Jesus' religion was an open system, pointing out toward life.

And yet Jesus did not leave Judaism. He faithfully used its form until the end. He went to synagogue (the rough equivalent of a parish church for Christians), he remained in the fellowship of religious people, he studied the Scriptures, and worshiped using its traditions. What he did was to use it well, freely, lightly, in a way that pointed not toward itself but toward life. And this is where it became a vital power for him and his disciples, in a way that threatened those who could only see religion as pointing in on itself.

Try to drop for a moment whatever assumptions you have about the Christian religion: what it teaches, what it demands, what it stands for. Instead, read through one of the Gospels and look at what Jesus himself asks of those with whom he comes in contact, how he points them back toward their lives: love

God with your thinking, feeling, acting, and with your soul; love every person because we are all children of God; name evil for what it is but love the evildoer; feed the hungry and help the suffering; don't be worried; turn to God in trust as soon as you are aware that you have separated yourself; know that underneath it all you are always one with God; be especially respectful of children and those who are outcasts; forgive people who hurt you; do not be attached to wealth; and be joyful and willing to suffer and die for this way of life because God is more powerful than hatred, fear, and death.

These words ring true for anyone who has ears to hear them, and they are about living life. This radical religious perspective was such a freeing experience that early Christians were willing to give up everything for it, even their lives. And when their leader died, they had an experience with him not of defeat but of victory and rebirth. Whatever one may say about the historicity of Jesus, his resurrection, and his teachings, we do know this: after his death, his followers were transformed from a small, powerless group into a large, free, and fearless one. They had been liberated by their experience with Jesus. They too had lost their religious limitations and gained faith. It caught on, and soon many others would also be liberated.

But by the early fourth century, the institutionalization of Christianity (brought to fulfillment by the Emperor Constantine) changed all that. Social and political pressure resulted in thousands joining up, and the institution grew. What was a way of living, a refreshing and liberating sense of the immediacy and love of God, now evolved into a *thing* again for many Christians. When it did, theology replaced experience. Jesus was set on a pedestal as an object. Requirements for legitimate membership, belief, and behavior crept in. What appeared again in large measure was a closed system, a cult. Instead of a reliance upon God-in-life, there was once more a reliance upon the form itself. Not all, of course, lived their faith this way. There have always been plenty of exceptions. Christian history is filled with examples of those who have shone with the radiance of Christ's freedom. But the legacy of Constantine has remained with us for far too long as we have continued to maintain the church as a closed system. And while cults promise the illusion of security, they get in the way of God-in-life.

THE CHURCH AS A CULT

T he church, like every institution, tends to gravitate toward what seems solid, permanent, and therefore secure. Without meaning to or even realizing what is happening, those who constitute the church substitute form—program, theology, disciplines, words and concepts of the faith—for the real thing. We become idolatrous.

  We create and cling to this closed system of security in many ways. We put artificial conditions, such as correct belief and behavior, upon God's presence in our lives as if we could control or prevent God's presence. We are taken away into pietism by preachers who smugly string together in-house words such as *grace, salvation, redemption, repentance,* and *community* and call it a sermon, never explaining what they mean. Neat, sophisticated theological formulae posit an abstract scenario of humankind's debt being magically wiped clean by a human/divine sacrifice, and we feel better knowing that this has taken place. We are told that others outside the closed system may appear to be happy and at peace, but that they are not really so. Events that happen to us, even senseless pain, are explained as being the result of God's will and part of an overall unseen plan. All of this creates the impression that the church possesses something mysterious and special that does not exist in the rest of life, and that if we as believers want to possess it, we too must adopt the closed system.

There is a dualism in this: the layering of a separate, special, spiritual world on top of our everyday one. What is offered is a false security that is self-decieving. It is not real. The map has been mistaken for the territory. We have forgotten that religion is merely a guide which points to life itself. No one looks at a map of the desert and assumes one has experienced what it is like to be in the desert. And yet we say the words and think the thoughts of religion's map, often believing that by doing this, we have the experience of God-in-life itself. T. S. Eliot is reported to have commented that the church is often like a sign in the window of a bakery that advertises: "Bread for sale: $1.00." But when we enter the store, we find that there is no bread. What is for sale is the sign.

Why did the early church move so inexorably toward becoming a closed system? Why does it continue to be so difficult for us to keep it open toward life, as Jesus did?

I believe it is because we are greedy and want to have things. We also fear life and therefore try to control it. The church often holds out, and the seeker embraces, a closed system because it offers the illusion that if we can create a religious alternative reality, we can own it, and therefore control it and be secure. Furthermore, it is painful, hard work to seek and be challenged by God in the moments of our ordinariness. And so we create an illusory, sacred reality that is supposed to be parallel to the secular one. It makes us feel better, at least superficially, to cling to this distraction. After all, it is more stimulating (for a while, at least) to be lost in a religious fervor of devotion to the Sacred Heart of Jesus than to sweep the floor prayerfully.

The church of former days, because of its tremendous power in Western society, used to be able to get away with this. But it can't anymore. We now live in a post-Christian age, which no longer takes the church and its teachings for granted.

The church has lost much of its influence. Not since Constantine (in the Western world) has it been so truly optional as to whether or not one should practice, or even keep up the appearance of practicing, the Christian faith. Unlike other times in history, there is currently no longer the assumption that one should take the church seriously. In fact, if one does, it is often deemed a bit odd. And so when we now function as a closed system instead of offering a liberating experience, people don't put up with it anymore. It doesn't make sense and so they just leave, turning to other paths.

I do not bemoan this fact. On the contrary, I see this as a positive development. Like the early church, Christianity is again in the position of being a real choice, rather than something that one does, at least half-heartedly and on occasion, as an expected prerequisite for being an upstanding citizen. As religiosity diminishes and pluralism expands in our culture, those who attend church will increasingly be those who follow the path of Jesus intentionally and seriously. The church may become smaller, but more focused.

A different response to this post-Constantinian situation has come out of the evangelical and fundamentalist perspectives, which see the world as an increasingly evil, sinking ship with the church as the only lifeboat that works. Christians are encouraged to get as many people to this lifeboat as soon as possible, before the whole thing goes down. Here the church is still a closed system, looking away from the risk and reward of the world's complexity and richness. Instead it relies exclusively upon the security and illusions of its own doctrine, rules, boundaries, community, and language. What this church resembles is again a cult, and this is fairly obvious to those outside of it. Christianity, of course, is not the only religion to manifest itself in fundamentalist separatism. Those who practice Judaism, Islam, and other religions with a fearful and closed attachment to the security of form do exactly the same thing. I am convinced that the fundamentalism of various faiths is really just one religion, serving the false idol of fear.

For progressive Christians, more attention needs to be paid to the manner in which we as individuals respond to this post-Constantinian age. Out of a desire for security in an increasingly uncertain time, we also create closed-system cults, in a more subtle way. A currently popular method is our attachment to what we call "spirituality." In various ways, we replace a radical openness to God-in-life with spiritual disciplines and programs. Spirituality is very fashionable these days, and to some degree this reflects an increasing dedication to holiness of life instead of religiosity. However, spirituality itself can become a thing, just like fundamentalism or institutionalism, when it turns away from life and toward itself.

Many spirituality programs offer some kind of focus upon certain disciplines: prayer, service to the poor, or study of the creeds and theology. These are all commendable, but an illusory desire for security often begins to creep in when the participants place their trust in external activities that are supposed to bring God "into" their life. Grasping to lay hold of a teacher, a conference, a book, a method of prayer, or a serious, disciplined rule of life that will finally get it all together for them, they cling to the hope for some magical change to come from without that will take them away from their life as it is and make them feel better.

The danger comes when we assume that if we do all of this according to the form provided, we will have had the experience itself. There is no such guarantee. There is no program that can replace the immediacy of God in thought, feeling, action; there is no form that can replace the sacred reality of whatever is before us this moment. Otherwise, the church becomes a closed system, a kind of idolatrous cult. Only this time, instead of the evangelical's cult of obedience to a literal interpretation of scripture, there is the cult of chasing after spiritual feelings that result from doing certain disciplines. Religion again becomes a thing, rather than an open system pointing out to and illuminating life.

Not everyone who uses programs of spirituality becomes idolatrous in this way, obviously. An example may help to distinguish between using the form of religion as a vehicle and believing in the form itself.

One person signs up for a spirituality program because he feels disconnected, overbusy, and vaguely empty. He hopes that by doing this he will find a way to move forward. He reads the Bible lessons assigned for reflection, thinks about their relation to his life, prays for guidance and insight, and starts volunteering at a shelter for the homeless. Meanwhile, his emptiness increases, only now it is even worse because he has the expectation that this program will change him. His emptiness continues because he is merely layering "spirituality" on top of his problems in the hope that it will help. He doesn't pay attention to his moments of boredom, his days of rage, his fears that keep him busy. Instead, he finds himself still caught in these things, and feels frustrated that they're still there. He prays for them to be taken away so he can be more spiritual. He turns his gaze to "God." He misses the opportunity to enter into the moments of his life with acceptance, patience, and reverence, knowing that God is there in the midst of it, knowing that true spirituality is being wherever we are, right now, in God. Instead, he looks to the form of religion and he is disappointed.

Disappointment is a helpful red flag. Usually it indicates that we have misplaced our hope in something that cannot and will not deliver what we thought it promised. This is what idolatry is all about: placing our trust in a false god which is false precisely because it won't do what it promises. For instance, we look for fulfillment and intimacy in the idol of lust, but lust can't deliver that. As Frederick Buechner says "Lust is a man in the desert, dying of thirst, eating salt." Our seeker has placed his trust in the idol of spirituality, which cannot deliver new life.

Another parishioner signs up for the spirituality program. This person is also, perhaps, feeling overbusy and vaguely empty. She also begins to read the Bible, to pray more regularly and help in an outreach ministry. But this parishioner makes no assumptions about what she is doing. Instead, she lets the spiritual disciplines and activities wash through her and trusts them to have whatever effect they will. But because she has taken on a form that is larger than herself, she begins to be able to get closer to the driving forces underneath her emptiness. She feels safe enough to enter into her pain because she is riding the supportive vehicle of religious community and discipline. She knows this vehicle will not save her, but it will be there to help carry her in her empty times. Now, when she feels the familiarity of disconnection, she rides through it and offers it back to God. She uses the form of religion as a vehicle, instead of believing in it as a thing.

The difference between our two parishioners is that one approaches religion as cult and the other uses it as a vehicle. The first attaches to the form and the second uses the form. Acting out of fear, the first actually places the form between him and his experience. The second uses it trustingly to open herself up to her life. The first wants to live in the form as a closed system. The second uses the form as an open system, pointing her back to what is. The first has made the form of religion an idol because he thinks it a real and permanent thing. The second recognizes religion's ephemeral nature—its imperfect effort to express the inexpressible—and she therefore takes it lightly. She knows what is real: her moments and her days in God.

WHERE DOES RELIGION COME FROM?

There is a big difference between believing in religion and using it as a form. At the heart of this difference lie our assumptions about the origin, nature, and purpose of religion. How do we think religious teaching and practice evolve? Some of those who rely upon it as a closed system, something permanent and real, would have us believe that the subjects of religion were communicated by God through people holier than we are, in a time holier than ours, in an accurate and unbiased fashion. They believe therefore that religion objectively reports on a spiritual reality that exists somewhere. Revelation here is seen in a fairly literal way. Just like I might reveal to you pictures and facts about my children, God long ago revealed pictures and facts about the divine.

Let's look at it from a different point of view. Imagine that twenty students are sitting in a classroom. Outside there is a terrible noise, and everyone rushes to the window. An airplane is falling out of the sky, and sure enough, it crashes right there in the field. Everyone sees it happen. All twenty rush outside and help rescue people. Amazing and heroic things happen as students rise above their normal level of functioning. They overcome their fear. A selfless spirit of compassion takes over. They all have this experience together. As a group, they are never the same. A new kind of community exists and people are transformed by the tragedy and by the greatness of their communal response.

After it is all over, these twenty different people tell the story of what happened in twenty different ways. Eventually a common story emerges, one that may not be factually true in the details, but which communicates the significance of what happened for the people involved. The story is so effective that it is told over several generations in the school. The story is shared not only as a way of reporting how individual and community lives were changed when it happened, but as a way of understanding how everyone can rise through fear and tragedy and reach compassionate greatness together.

The story is, at this point, after the fact. It is only a picture of what originally happened to and in those people in the past.

The experience itself was real, and even though the story is true and grounded in the real event, it is not real in the same sense. The story of the plane crash and the rescue is now a picture, a vehicle, but it is not the experience itself. But it points to and even helps people know something real for themselves: the human experience of tragedy, compassion, and self-transcendence. As people go through these real things in their own life, they even participate in the reality which the original plane crash witnesses went through. The story, however inaccurate in its details, served to unite people's experience in the past and present.

Why should it be any different for the Bible, or for theology? These were ordinary human beings who had an extraordinary experience that was very real. They did not make it up. But they did have to find ways of communicating it so that those who heard their story might be led into the same experience. In telling the story, they used the only tools they had: the symbols, language, and concepts of their time and place. While their experience, and eventually our own parallel experience, is very real, the story is not real, in the same sense. The story is a picture which at its best only points us back to our experience.

Our picture of Jesus from the Gospels is like this. Jesus of Nazareth was a real man. He had an experience of God-in-life that was extraordinary. Others around him were utterly transformed by God in Jesus' presence. After he was gone from them, they looked around and said to themselves, "Who and what was that?" They had to find a way of trying to put the experience into words. They had to paint a picture so that others might be transformed as they were. Being men of the first-century Greek and Jewish world of the Mediterranean, they used the colors and textures that were familiar to them in order to make this picture. They used terms and symbols that were already commonly used like *Redemption*, *Salvation*, *Son of God*, *Messiah*, *the Word*, and *the Christ*. These words even appeared as Jesus' own when the faith community, now a generation later, recollected and wrote down the experience of their elders.

The picture that resulted was one of its own time and place. It was expressed in the only form that was possible then and there. The picture continues to be so compelling, however, that it still has the power to do what the authors intended: it can awaken in the beholder, even in the present-day, the very experience that they had two thousand years ago. Again, their (and our) experience was (and is) transformative and real. But the picture used to communicate this reality is time-bound, limited, expressive: It is not a real thing.

The problem comes when the picture is taken for the real thing, when the finger pointing to the moon is mistaken for the moon itself. Then this picture of Jesus is held up as some kind of thing, objectively frozen in this form for all eternity. When this picture is removed from experience, the church holds up this frozen thing and asks us to believe in it, whatever that means. Without connecting with our real life experience, we say that we "believe in" "the Only Son of God" who "came down" from "heaven," who now "sits at the right hand of the Father," will "come again in glory" in order to "be our judge." We attach certain images in our minds to these statements of creed, and believe that these images are factual descriptions of an objective reality.

We often forget that those who originally committed these statements to paper were trying to express their common experience of God in Christ, not certain immutable facts that described an alternate religious reality, handed down from heaven. The Scriptures, the Creeds, and other forms of theology developed slowly as people began to ask themselves what it was like to live in God in this new way. All of the theology of the church has emerged out of people's reflection upon their real life experience.

While the authors of these creedal statements may have been expressing their real, extraordinary, transformative experience in their own contemporary terms, what do *we* mean when we recite them? Is the Creed merely a list of intellectual assertions about God and Jesus' nature to which we must hold if we are to be a part of the Christian group? It's not that reciting these things is wrong; I happen to believe them. But when these forms are disassociated from experience and held onto like some inviolate holy thing, they actually prevent us from having the experience that they are supposed to communicate. The Creed as a statement of frozen assertions is deadening.

On the other hand, the particular form of the gospel and the creedal picture of Jesus which we have inherited is an extremely powerful vehicle when allowed to be just that. The Creed becomes a living document when seen as an expression of human experience. For me, to "believe" in Jesus is to stake my life on his way as the way that will free me, just like it freed his disciples. To call Jesus "the Only Son of God" is to see that his way is the one universal way, expressed in many forms, that all who seek God's life must tread. It is to also recognize Jesus' unity with God, which he claims we can know as well. Saying he "came down from heaven" is to say that "when I follow Jesus' way, I am relying upon a power that comes to me, that is more transcendent than my individual smallness." To say that he "sits at the right hand of the Father" is to know that this experience he brings to me is universal and crosses all boundaries of time, religion, personality, and geography. Jesus "comes in glory to be our judge" because when his way manifests itself with clarity, love, and power in my life, I am brought to the truth, which sets me free.

WHAT, THEN, OF BELIEF?

If religion is a culturally biased expression of subjective human experience, what is there left to believe in? If religion is simply a vehicle for working with our own individual, subjective experience, how can or why should different people hold a common belief?

The temptation with an experience-based religion is to approach it as a kind of spiritual smorgasbord. This is to say that all practices, all beliefs, are available and of equal value and effect. We can pick and choose whatever we want for our plates and any combination of things will end up with the same result. Furthermore, since all religion emerged from imperfect human sources, the truths of religion are interchangeable with any other truths we may have discovered or even made up on our own. In fact, this extreme subjective approach would say that all beliefs, traditions, theologies, and practices are really the same. This is not so.

The Aztec practice of ripping the hearts out of prisoners-of-war as they screamed on the altar of Huitzilopochtli is clearly not the same as loving one's enemy. Chanting "God is Great" as one drives a car-bomb into a crowd is not the same as seeking "Allah, the Compassionate, the Merciful" in the practice of the religion of Islam (which literally means "peace"). Some religious beliefs and practices are harmful and others are helpful. It is not enough to say, "If it is true for you, then, in fact, it is true." It is not enough to say that religion simply expresses and leads us back into subjective experience. After all, it is possible to be lost and harmful to others in our subjective experience. Religion is also about objective truth.

Objective truth is not about some set of ideas or beliefs. It is not about possessing something that others do not have. It is not about figuring out a philosophy that is logical, consistent, and correct. Objective truth is simply the way things are. Gravity causes things to be drawn toward the earth. Life works that way. If a marriage partner lies and cheats on her spouse, trust will be broken and the marriage will suffer. New trees in the forest grow out of dead composted material. That's just the way it is.

In the same way, religion that is useful expresses and leads one back into objective truth, objective reality. For instance, I think that our dependence upon one another and God is an objective religious truth. If we try to go it alone in growing spiritually, relying upon the supreme effort of our will power, we will fail. If we try to accomplish, on our own, the heights of consciousness, it won't work. At some point we must find out that surrender is necessary. Sooner or later, we find that true strength lies in our weakness. This is just the way we are made. In fact, it is the way everything is made. Nothing in the universe exists in self-sufficiency. All is reliant upon everything else, and all is reliant upon God, the source of life. That's just the way we, and all things, are made.

I also think that it is an objective religious truth that peace of mind can only be found by dying to our attachments and fears, and living to God. If we believe that we will find peace by accumulating things, by avoiding suffering and chasing pleasure, we will not succeed. Eventually the emptiness of possessions and pleasure will betray us. Our attempts to protect ourselves from what we fear will lead to greater insecurity. It won't work. If we are seekers, we will discover that new life comes out of death. We will find that only by being aware of, and dying to, our attachments, will we know freedom. We will find that only by entering into our fears and letting ourselves experience them will we be released from them and enter into a firmer foundation for real freedom. No one was ever made happy by chasing pleasure and avoiding pain. Resurrection really does come after dying to self. That's just the way we are made.

It is also objectively true that compassion and justice create harmony, just as hatred and oppression create violence. This is the way people are made. It is objectively true. We can choose to ignore this fact, but we will reap the consequences. To see but one example, one need only look at the continuing consequences of Latin America's long and sad history of Spanish and North American domination through military, political, religious, and economic oppression. For centuries, those in power have pushed against the created order of love and justice, and the result is now widespread poverty, violence, pollution, frustration, and rage.

What does this have to do with Christian belief in God or Jesus? When we say we believe in God, we are saying that it is objectively true that there is a permeating force of life and goodness in all living things, and that in this sense we are not alone. This is not just a nice idea, conveniently chosen. It is an experience of reality, and we depend upon the objective truth of this experience for our life. When we say we believe in God, we are saying that God's love in us really does conquer hatred. This is not just a concept that is interchangeable with other concepts. It is what we believe to be true about life, and we stake our life upon it.

When we say that we believe in Jesus, we are saying that the way he lived is the way anyone must live if we they are to know peace of mind. We are saying that only by loving the marginalized, dying to attachments (including, ultimately, our own life), and seeking God's immediate presence in all situations as Jesus did, can a person be truly free. Belief in Jesus is not simply an agreement with certain assertions about him. It is a belief that his is the way, truly and objectively, to life. It is a belief that his way is the way humans are made to be. It is a belief that his way works.

Belief is not intellectual. It is the discovery of life itself, the way it truly is. As we discover the way things are, we know what we can trust and what we can't trust. And when we place our trust in what we have discovered, we are really believing. It must be remembered that the New Testament word for faith is a verb. We don't "have" faith in some *thing* such as an image of God or Jesus. We *faith*. We *faith* in what we have discovered really works. We *faith* in what we know is objectively true about life.

Religion, if it is to be useful, must point the way to the objective truths it has discovered over time that lead to life. It must speak of human/divine experience in a way that awakens one to the true reality of God-in-life. It must provide practices and disciplines that really work, that really bring freedom and peace of mind. It must model compassion and justice so that people may move from a belief in the idea of a loving God to an experience of the objective truth of God's ever-present love. Religion does not have to be a closed system, a dualistic cult that protects and distracts its adherents from reality. Religion can be an open system, pointing outward. It can be a vehicle which takes one into the richness of life, transforming those who use it well.

2

Using the Christian Form

We have this treasure in earthen vessels,
so that it may be made clear that this extraordinary power
belongs to God and does not come from us.
— Paul (2 Cor. 4:7)

*F*or many in our age, using the Christian form as one's spiritual vehicle is not an easy thing. We often have considerable personal baggage attached to theological terms: visual symbols, the name of Jesus Christ, even the word "God." Add to this our contemporary culture's general lack of confidence in any kind of institution and its traditions, and the tentative, borderline Christian may have a significant challenge if he wants to enter trustingly into the Christian form and use it well.

However, some who choose to deal with their ghosts will be able to unmask false interpretations that they inherited from others, and claim it on their own terms. This is no small feat; it requires courage and some kind of persistent attraction.

Nevertheless, in spite of these difficulties, the Christian way offers much for those who use it well. Here, within this form, is the story of a human life that is surrounded by all-too familiar political oppression, greed, and narrow-mindedness; in the midst of this he moves faithfully in love toward God-in-life, and in so doing he reveals evil and suffering to be paper tigers. Here is the recurring image of a divine force that reaches through life into all circumstances, healing, and enlightening what is open to it. Here is a long lineage of witnesses to a way of life that is free and full of love. Here is a group of ordinary people willing to challenge and stick with one another until something breaks open and a holy community begins to be formed by a power outside of and yet within it. What more do we need?

The one who seeks to use the Christian tradition will inevitably have to do so, in part, in a congregation of some kind. Community, after all, has always been the locus of the tradition, the means by which its life has emerged, evolved, been expressed and handed down. When a seeker enters the local congregation, there are three primary ways in which the Christian form is presented, three vehicles through which the life of God in Christ is expressed: in scripture, theology, and liturgy. There is no escaping these three expressions, for everywhere we look they are evident. In sacramental churches the place is virtually dripping with them.

Scripture's stories are found in stained-glass windows, readings, hymns, the liturgical year, and in the conversational allusions that frame members' life events. Theology is found in sermons, prayers, creeds, commentary on social issues, and in the way people understand what is happening to them. Liturgy is the symbolic drama into which a Sunday seeker will enter and find oneself again and again; it is the medium through which the people relate most profoundly to one another in God. Scripture, theology, and liturgy are the ways in which the church presents its form, and also the ways in which the seeker grapples with the same. How can we use them well, to serve an experiential, authentic faith?

TELLING STORIES

*F*or the borderline Christian, an uninformed hearing of scripture while sitting vulnerably in the pew on a Sunday morning may have disastrous effects. Some awful passage is read with great reverence, something about how God doesn't reveal truth to any other nation but Israel, or how women should be subject to men, or how evil the world is. Heard out of context, with no introduction or explanation, the tentative Christian is thrown back into her religious trauma, wondering what on earth she is doing there. Assuming that she cannot simply close her ears every time scripture is read in church, what kind of general approach should she take?

One common approach that will not help is to take everything literally. This may seem obvious, but an explanation may assist in moving quickly beyond this popular method of reading scripture. To take the Bible at face value, without criticism or evaluation, is to pretend a simplicity in the authorship and an objectivity in our reading, neither of which really exist. It may be appealing to some to put a bumper sticker on their car that says "The Bible Says It, I Believe it, and That Settles It!" but this simple statement overlooks certain realities. Whatever the Bible "says" in one passage, it often says the opposite of somewhere else. To "believe" what we read without question is to assume that on first reading, we know, in fact, what was intended two thousand years ago when it was written to a different audience with a cultural and historical setting far removed from our own.

Let's take the handful of passages in scripture where homosexuality is condemned. To read these literally, one might assume that A) scripture is clear about the confining of sexual activity to marriage, and B) scripture's condemnation applies to gay and lesbian couples today as much as it did in Sodom and Gomorrah. But to read it in this way is to overlook other conflicting messages in the Bible, such as Jesus' acceptance of those deemed "unclean" by others and scripture's acceptance of polygamy. A literal reading also overlooks the fact that the historical circumstances of pagan temple prostitution, promiscuous

Roman bath house pedophilia, and attempted gang rape of those in Sodom all played a crucial role in defining just what kind of sin was being condemned. A God-centered, monogamous lesbian couple seeking the church's blessing for their adopted daughter is quite another story. We often twist scripture around our own preconceptions and prejudices when we claim "The Bible Says it, I Believe it, and That Settles It!"

Another approach to scripture that is equally unhelpful is the search for passages that will make us feel good, and the subjective application of those passages to our own circumstances. Here we avoid those difficult passages that annoy or confound us, preferring instead to focus on those that remind us of what we already know to be important and good. The pitfalls of this approach are obvious; while this method may make us feel better, we will never learn anything by it, and in fact we may only be reinforcing our ignorance. Yet it is amazing to see how popular this method of using scripture is.

For example, there is much in scripture about love; how we should love our enemies, return love for hatred, and hold only love in our hearts. Let's say someone in a position of power in our workplace is an oppressive, mean person. An emotional, subjective reading of these passages on love may comfort us and keep us quiet. A subjective application of them may support our already held view that the only real spiritual answer is to be kind to him and pray for him. While this may in fact partially help our workmate, our subjective application of scripture manages to overlook its long tradition of prophetic justice, Jesus' strength and anger in the face of wrong, and the clear call to be people of risk in the cause of the oppressed.

An approach to the use of scripture that *will* help is a contextual one. Three specific contexts will help us both to understand and use what we read.

First of all, this kind of reading takes the original context, as much as we are able to know about it, into consideration.

Who wrote it? To whom? What was the purpose of the writing? What cultural and historical trends were influencing the author? Is it mystical poetry, correspondence, heroic story, or personal witness? While the reader may not know the answer to these questions, others do, and just asking these kinds of questions will begin to open up the possibilities.

Secondly, the Bible should be seen in context of the overall themes of scripture. Is this consistent with the broad truths of the rest of scripture's authors (who embody a significant amount of spiritual experience?) Or is it a minor, superceded view that has, therefore, less authority for Christians?

Finally, for the one seeking an experiential faith, the passage under consideration should be reflected upon in the context of one's life. Does this apply to me? How do I feel about it? If I'm uncomfortable, is it because I'm trying to avoid something that needs examination, or am I simply trying to redeem a passage that has, let's say, more to do with destructive patriarchy than the love of God? What, if anything, does this scripture call me to do, to become?

Asking these kinds of questions will put scripture itself in its proper context. The Bible is not God. It is a collection of stories and teachings told by an ancient people concerning their experience with God. Sometimes they were wrong, and sometimes they were right on the money. This point of view will make some nervous ("Well, if we can pick and choose what to believe, what good is it?"). But it will also return ultimate truth to where it belongs: to God. God will highlight and burn in our souls from scripture what we need to hear and heed. God will use this imperfect, human document (what other kind of material does God have to work with in this human life, anyway?) to awaken us to the miracle of our life. God will use teachers, friends, books, and the Spirit within to sort out what is eternally true from what is culturally misguided in scripture.

On the other hand, as people of the biblical tradition, we take the Bible seriously. For we recognize that it represents centuries of broad experience, an experience of thousands of people, many of whom were utterly devoted to and graced by God in profound ways. This representation far outweighs the limited experience of our own individual lives. While we may have more wisdom than one or another of the particular voices of scripture, we cannot make this claim about the broad themes and recurring truths that shine through its human limitations.

While we take scripture seriously, we must also give ourselves permission to have some perspective on it; it's all right for scripture to anger, awaken, bore, annoy, delight, confuse, inspire, and leave us feeling neutral. All of scripture doesn't have to be enlightening. To treat all of the Bible as a kind of divine object that we are supposed to grimly revere, even if it seems way out of whack with our own experiences is to give it an oppressive authoritarianism that its authors did not intend.

With a contextual approach to scripture we allow it to be for us what it is: a varied collection of inspired beauty, misguided delusion, paradoxical mystery, spiritual immaturity, and divine wisdom. With this attitude we can take it lightly or seriously, with humor or reverence, as the text demands. Most importantly, we can trust that the same God who spoke to the authors and characters of scripture, real people in time and place, will also guide us through its use and speak to us in our own time and place.

IMAGING GOD

*J*ust as the Bible is not God, neither is the church's theology. Like scripture, theology is a people's record of their experience with God, not a description of objective reality that has been

handed down to us from on high. Nevertheless, theology is a
useful thing, because, like scripture, it can express the collective wisdom of many people whose experience and intelligence is far wider than our own as individuals. Again, the
church's traditional theology should be taken seriously, but
with some perspective. Only God is God, and as a preaching
professor used to say "The tools of theologians are forever
breaking in their hands."

Theology is most useful when it is looked at in an experiential way. In order to use its form well, we must ask: how did
this or that theology emerge from the real-life experience of
those who set it forth, and how does it speak to my experience?
To demonstrate an experiential approach to scripture, let's take
an extended look at what is perhaps the key doctrine of the
Christian faith, the doctrine of the Trinity.

Father

ALL PEOPLE OF THE WORLD, in one way or another, find
themselves awakened to the sheer majesty of the universe.
The ancient people of Israel, Mayan temple builders, prophets,
yogis, shepherds, the children surrounding Jesus, as well as
you and I, all have moments when we are made aware of the
transcendence, beauty, and mystery of creation. These moments change us. They bring us peace in the midst of tur-
moil, because by them we are reminded that we are not
limited by the prison of present circumstances. These moments draw us forward to move through our fears and our
self-imposed limitations so that we can become something
higher than before.

We also have moments when we seem to be helped by a
power beyond ourselves. Just when we are the most confused,
just when we have no will or ability to save ourselves, clarity
and purpose from beyond reach out and pull us forward. The
alcoholic has no power to stop drinking, but when she gives up

and surrenders to something beyond herself, she miraculously has the power to stop. When meditating, an open and graceful awareness comes precisely when we reach the bitter end of our frustrating efforts to get there on our own.

And then there are those often painful times when we are given the ability to truly see ourselves, beneath our pretenses and illusions about the self. We are revealed for who we are and who we are not. We face what we have done and what we have not done. We are judged by the truth. These times are not always loaded with emotion, either positive or negative, for judgment and truth are not ultimately about feeling: they are about what is. If it is done with compassion, we see ourselves with simple acceptance, without self-loathing or sentimental affection. We simply see. This kind of judgment is merely naming the facts.

These moments of self-transcendence, of help, and of judgment are universal experiences. Everyone, if they are open to life, comes across them. They are not of our own making, although they may involve our effort. They come from the source of all life and healing. They come from God. And so the Israelites and the early church gave a name to this experience of life, of God. They called God Father, using an image that was familiar, using the materials of language that lay at hand to paint a picture of their experience. The name Father was given for this experience of God because for a child, a parent at his or her best is a transcendent creator, helping and compassionately judging.

When we call upon God as Father or Mother, we are leaning upon transcendence. We are leaning upon the source of creation and the force that animates all of life. When we call upon the Mother or the Father, we also are asking for help from the source of all goodness. We recognize that we must surrender in weakness in order for a strength that is beyond us to be ours. When we call upon the Father or the Mother of us all, we are also inviting transcendent truth. We are asking to be judged by criteria that are not of our own making, for we often deceive ourselves. We are asking for our condition as it is to be named so that we can see it, accept it and move beyond it. Such is our desire for God the Father, God the Mother.

Son

THERE ARE TIMES when this sense of the transcendence, help, and judgment are localized in a human form. People of the world have always recognized certain individuals as special, as holy. That is why every culture has priests, shamans, spiritual masters, and teachers. Hopefully (but not always) it is because these individuals have been recognized by others as being clear, loving, and wise. Some people have a presence about them that, just by being around them, makes real for us the wonder of life. Suddenly what has up until now only been interior, stands before us, in the flesh. We can see that the life we long for is possible, because we can directly relate to the one who stands before us. They are filled with God's wisdom and love and in that sense they are one with God, for they share one nature.

Jesus, son of Joseph and Mary, a young Jewish carpenter from the small town of Nazareth, had such a presence. Jesus was no ordinary man. He was in such unity with God that the divine was transparently visible through him. People dropped everything in order to follow him, for in his presence they found peace. His teachings were understandable (although not acceptable) to all. He loved everyone, especially those whom others would reject. His touch healed people of disease and emotional illness (which was often diagnosed then as demonic possession). He was given a power through his unity with God so that, at times, he defied the laws of nature. He was transparent to God even through his betrayal, suffering, and death. Finally, his friends experienced him as transcending even death. Jesus continued somehow to be alive for them.

This experience of God was so concrete, so astoundingly real, that God was no longer seen by those around Jesus only as the transcendent creator, helper, and judge. God was now experienced also as a friend who was like them. God was now experienced as one who appeared to them in a form that they could understand. And so they used language which was at hand in order to paint a picture of this experience. Those who were Jewish called him Messiah, the expected Anointed One: the servant of God who would lead Israel into peace. Those who were Greek called him what they knew through their philosophy: the Logos (the Word), or animating force of wisdom which has been a part of creation since the beginning. They could only describe their experience of God in Jesus through concepts and images that were of their time and place.

Eventually the early church gave a name to this experience of God in Jesus: The Son. A son or a daughter represents the parents from whom they originated. They are one with their parents in the sense that they resemble them, they carry forth their legacy, they even share their genes and their blood. Jesus was for the early church the Son of God because he carried forth God's being.

But this concrete experience of God which Jesus lived and enabled for others manifests itself in many other forms as well. It is a universal experience. Wherever transcendent holiness, compassionate help, and the judging truth are present in people, God is incarnated. All seekers of the world who find the wonder, love, and truth of creation enfleshed before them truly encounter the same energy that flowed through Jesus. In many ways, God is experienced as Son, as one who is concrete, human, and understandable.

And so when I speak of Jesus Christ as being the savior of all, as eternal and as one being with God, I do not speak only of Jesus of Nazareth. I speak of the universal experience of God which manifested itself completely in Jesus of Nazareth. I speak of the energy which not only flowed through him but through others, which is personal, concrete, salvific, eternal, and divine. This energy is always the same, no matter what form it takes on. It is always the enfleshing, saving presence of God in human form. In this sense there is only one Son of God. It may have different forms, but it is one reality.

When Christians call upon God the Son, we are asking that God be incarnated in human situations. We ask that the wisdom and love which Jesus had be ours as well. We name him Lord and thereby remind ourselves that the center of our values, our intentions, and hopes is the life which Jesus presented. When we call upon Christ, we are expressing our desire to become like him and that we be given the ability to see him in other people. When we call upon Christ to save us, we ask that we too may become one with God in the same way that Jesus was, so that we can become whole as he was whole.

Spirit

WHEN WE MOVE our awareness of God from creator of the universe to the one who is incarnated in holy men and women, we have moved a little closer to ourselves. But this is not close enough. People have also always had an experience with an even more intimate sense of the divine: within one's own heart and mind.

Some years ago in Santa Fe a conference was being planned which was to include practitioners of various religious traditions: Native American, Buddhist, Christian, Jewish, Islamic, and others. In the leaders' planning, they recognized the need to center around a religious experience that was familiar to all traditions. This theme was to be the common ground for the participants in the conference. They decided to use the breath.

The Jewish people long ago knew that the breath was holy. Their word for it was *ruach*, which was the same word for both wind and the Spirit of God. Because the breath is the very source of life in the moment, the act of taking a breath is to experience creation. We breathe in God's life and we are alive.

When this ceases, our bodies die. Native Americans have the same awareness of breath and God's presence. Christians have forms of contemplative prayer which attend to the breath as the locus of our life in God. Buddhists do not often speak of God, but their meditation practice is often centered in the concrete act of the breath. For many Buddhists, the more one is awake to the breath, the more one is awake to the spontaneous wonder of life.

If the breath is truly the place where we discover the fundamental act of creation in the moment, surely it is nothing less than the presence of God. Like the breath, God moves into our body, our mind, and our heart in the simple act of being alive, in the act of being a creature of the creator. In each moment, God, like the breath, animates our thinking, our physical movements, our emotions, and our spiritual knowing.

It was this experience of God's animating intimacy which the Jewish people called Wisdom. An entire book of the same name from the Old Testament Apocrypha is dedicated to this experience. Many of the Psalms, the Proverbs, and much of the book of Ecclesiastes are about Wisdom. Wisdom is a quality which emanates from God, which has always been and always will be present with God. Wisdom is also active as God's living force in all aspects of creation. It is a feminine quality, and referred to by feminine pronouns in scripture. She is known as the experience of God that gives life, meaning, insight, and direction. Happy is the one who follows her bidding.

Surely this Wisdom is the same as the Holy Spirit, which is identified as a gift from God to Christians of the early church in the New Testament. Here, the Holy Spirit is also the giver of new life, meaning, direction, and insight. In both cases, what is described is essentially a feminine force. She is intuitive, interior, nourishing, forceful, and transformative. It is, in my mind, a tragic loss to history that the theologians of the early church did not directly identify the third person of the Trinity as Wisdom. But they were products of their own patriarchal society. Had they spoken of the Father, the Son, and the Wisdom of God, we would have a more balanced Trinity. The Father could carry the masculine energy (which both women and men possess) of creative external action, judgment, and transcendent power. Wisdom could carry the feminine energy (also common to men and women alike) of the internal stirring of the soul, intuition, and the strength of endurance. All of these masculine and feminine characteristics are qualities of God, and since we are made in God's image, they are also qualities of women and men.

Whenever I say the Nicene Creed in liturgical worship, I substitute the pronoun "she" for "he" when speaking of the Holy Spirit. For those in the church who use pronouns when referring to God, perhaps it is time to start actively using the feminine pronoun, and a good place to start is with the Holy Spirit, the Wisdom of God.

Whenever we call upon the Holy Spirit, we are calling upon God, for she is as close to us as our own breath. She is within us. When we call upon the Holy Spirit, we are invoking the animating force of life that blows mysteriously through every particle in the universe, through every living cell and every exploding star. Whenever we call upon the Holy Spirit, we are asking for her to nurture and guide us into all truth.

In like fashion, we may examine any of the church's traditional theology: the Incarnation, Salvation, Grace, Forgiveness, or Creation. The kinds of questions that we will ask if seeking an experiential understanding are: What is the universal human experience to which this particular theological form points? Are there other traditions that use similar theological form to express this universal reality? What kind of experience did the people have from whom this theology emerged? How can I look at my experience to get into this theology in a way that brings it alive for me?

In the end, theology is just a form as well, a form that can only hint at what cannot be described in mere words. But as such it may point us in a direction that will help, a direction that will lead us further into the mystery of God.

THE CHURCH AT PLAY

In order to use the Christian form well, we will have to find a way of making its worship our own. My understanding of how this normally takes place is through some kind of surrender, some act of trust in the liturgy. The borderline Christian may not be able to do this at first, but over time, if she has worked with the scripture contextually (especially those types of scripture that are most difficult for her), and if she has taken an experiential approach to theology, liturgy will become integrated and therefore easier to trust. Eventually, liturgy becomes a familiar dance into which one steps and is carried along by the group, by the actions, the music, and the weight of history. In surrendering one's whole being to this dance, we are taken further into God's life.

However, until we have integrated its language and become accustomed to its rhythm, dramatic structure, and recurring themes, we will trip over our feet and distract ourselves by the details as they sail by us. Even those of us who have integrated the liturgy will admit, if we are honest with ourselves, that we are not very good dancers. Most of the time our conscious mind only hears one or two things in an hour of worship. The remainder of the time our minds are somewhere else. We find ourselves thinking of the events of the coming afternoon, or whether we remembered to feed the cats that morning.

But not to worry. Over the years, we hear it all. That makes it possible to let the liturgy wash through us on a weekly basis, knowing that its teachings and truth will gradually sink in more deeply over time. When we attend Eucharist, we must, just as in prayer, set our intention, offer ourselves where we are, and then let go of the rest. We can trust that God will do with our offering what needs to be done. It needn't be known to us, it needn't be felt. The conscious mind isn't everything. In fact it is only a small part of our being. We should not underestimate what goes on in our depths. It is enough to do the act of intention, surrender, and reception. The rest is up to God, the source of all life and renewal.

The word *liturgy* is a Greek one, originally used to describe the worship life of the church. Literally, this word means "the work of the people." I prefer to think of it as play.

Children know how to do liturgy. Their habitual play is a way of ordering life, creating symbolic acts that can carry them forward through what seems like, at time, random chaos. Tirelessly, children repeat the same story, accompanied by the same actions, over and over. In fact, they insist that the story be repeated in exact form and will correct the storyteller who attempts to vary it. This is because they need to create liturgy for themselves in order to make symbolic, psychic meaning. They work out deep emotional battles through mythic characters that they invent. Evil, goodness, courage, and hope are the themes of their play. But while it is often very serious in its intent, children's play can be light in its execution.

Liturgical worship is the same. The parish community gathers together, usually weekly, and we play. We use symbolic words, actions, costumes, special music, habitual greetings, a predictable order, and repeated phrases. Our liturgical play is a way of surrendering to a structure that can carry our deep, subconscious forces into relationship with our Creator, who can then work with them. Darkness and light, guilt, eternity, grief, and joy are all carried along and transformed by the play which we make.

We don't even understand what we are doing, but we know that in this play something is stirring that needs to be stirred.

In the play we offer these deep interior forces, but we also receive other forces, at a level beneath our understanding. We are touched by symbol, God, community, and story. An interchange takes place of which we are not in control. This is the power of liturgy, and this is why it can be either so moving or so infuriating. There is nothing better than being lifted up inside oneself to a heightened awareness of God, shared by everyone in the room. There is nothing worse than a manipulative preacher who seizes upon the deep emotions of a crowd to fulfill his own needs and foist his own agenda.

Liturgical worship is most real when we come at it like children. Dealing with serious issues that are way beyond our conscious understanding, we play with lightness and flexibility. We know it is important, this play, but we do not take ourselves too seriously when doing it. While order and repetition are helpful, the little quirks given by forgetting whole sections of the rite or children's shouted exclamations are part of the play as well. While we work to maintain an atmosphere of reverence and transcendent grace, we do so with a wink of the eye. Self-important, serious liturgy kills the spirit.

What happens when we surrender ourselves to this dance, this corporate play? For one thing, it is a way to see our connection with other people, places, and times. We can extend the boundaries of the self. Sitting right next to a stranger who may be at the opposite end of the social scale from us, we play together as sisters and brothers in God. Praying for those who are oppressed in Africa or Tibet, we can see our link with distant people across economic and political barriers. Asking for the prayers of the saints who lived in centuries past, we join them in our common, eternal existence in God. Praying for those who are sick in the community, we move out of our isolated self-absorption. Seeing a bishop in cope, miter, and crozier, we remember the connection we have through the laying on of hands which extends back through history, person to person, touch to touch, to Jesus himself. Playing in a liturgical form that is historic and worldwide in use, we are taken out of the confines of time and place. In liturgy, we stretch out and beyond our little self-contained unit.

When we play in liturgy, we also mark time. When there is a birth, death, marriage, divorce, new job, or adoption, it is good to mark the moment. The profound influence of these and other events upon our lives should not be underestimated. We become different people as the events of life affect us. Liturgy helps us simply to acknowledge this fact and to hold these events before God, asking for them to be filled with grace. The cycles of the liturgical year are further ways that we enter into time. Christmas, for instance, is primarily concerned with Jesus' birth and its corresponding significance for us. But the church, in her worldly wisdom, set the date for this feast conspicuously close to that of the pre-Christian festival of the winter solstice. We thus celebrate the victory of light over darkness in more ways than one. Similarly, Easter (near the spring equinox) is partly a celebration of spring and the regeneration of the earth. In liturgy, we mark the time, honoring the effects of its passage.

Through the yearly or weekly presentation of certain repeated themes, liturgical worship also teaches. These thematic foci drive home the truths to which they point. Death and resurrection are natural facts of daily life which we must learn to recognize and cooperate with, and so every year we act out Good Friday and Easter, in order to imbed this truth. We belong to each other and to God, and so every time there is a baptism we celebrate it together, publicly, with vows of support and a renewal of commitment. God lives within us like a fire, and so we observe the annual feast of Pentecost. We are one with all those who seek God, and so we celebrate All Saints'

Day. We separate ourselves from God regularly, and so each week, and particularly during the season of Lent, we repent, turning back to the unity of love which we share with God. Every feast and fast, every season of the church brings us back to something that is good for us to remember and practice throughout the year. Our skulls are thick enough to require annual, if not weekly, repetition. As we play liturgically with these Christian themes, over time we slowly learn to practice them in our lives. This kind of learning is not intellectual; it is experiential. Walking through the same territory, visiting the same themes, over and over, year after year, we are eventually immersed in the truth of the faith, and this truth changes our outlook and behavior.

Most importantly, however, when we do liturgical play we bring our life as it is with us, and we offer it back to its source. An exchange takes place. We receive something from God and we go away with a different perspective. We remember to stop and give thanks. We pause before the majestic beauty and sadness of it all. We watch ourselves from God's point of view and see the silly worries and busyness with which we consume ourselves. Our heart opens, and we become vulnerable to something that is clear, expansive, and real. Perhaps we become more able to embrace our suffering, to move through it and even appreciate it. We might see someone who annoys us as a fellow child of God and give them what they need the most: acceptance. Maybe we'll write our senator, start a food pantry, or work for the dignity and rights of the marginalized. Perhaps we will slow down and look at the sky.

There are no guarantees in attending worship. If we are not seeking the experience of the living God in our lives, then nothing is going to happen in the Eucharist. If we can't perceive God at home while taking the garbage out or while on the telephone at work, we won't see God in the incense and stained glass window. Worship is vital only if we are awake to

God in our lives. In this sense liturgy becomes a mirror of where we are at any given time. When we are happy, liturgy seems joyful. When we are alienated, it all seems foreign and strange. When we are depressed, it seems oppressive. When we are at peace, it seems transcendent. Using this form of Christian tradition well then becomes a matter of offering what we are, on any given day, back to our source, and trusting that the church, through this form, will carry us into the presence of God.

•

WE DO INDEED have this sacred treasure, our life in God, in earthen vessels. We are creatures of the earth, fallible, limited, and broken. Our institutions, our history, our traditions, and any religious forms that we corporately develop over time will inevitably be just as fallible, limited, and broken as we are. Even though we may be terribly disappointed in this inevitable fact, earthen vessels are all we are ever going to have as creatures of the earth. There is no other more perfect vessel elsewhere in this life. But through this cracked and crumbling vessel a sacred treasure, a divine light struggles to enlighten. And it does.

The primary form of Christian tradition—the scripture, theology, and liturgy of the church—is not the only earthen vessel that carries God's light. Nor should it be mistaken for the light itself. But it is a good vessel, one that has emerged out of considerable pain, joy, and wisdom. It is one of the most significant fruits of this vast world's contemplation of her immeasurable Creator. Happy are those who are called to use it, and use it well.

3

Letting God Grow Up

When I was a child, I spoke as a child, I thought as a child,
I reasoned like a child; when I became an adult
I put an end to childish ways. For now we see in a
mirror, dimly, but then we will see face to face.
Now I know only in part; then I will know fully,
even as I have been fully known.
—Paul (1 Cor. 13:11–12)

*T*hose who seek an experiential, life-centered faith will inevitably come up against their image of God. Baggage from the past will haunt us here more than in any other place in our religion, for our image of God begins in the subconscious and is therefore elemental. Unless we recognize how we received this image and where we might have become stuck along the way, we will never mature in our faith, and God will not become alive in new ways within our life. How then does an image of God evolve, and how does it keep evolving? How do we grow spiritually, and how does that growth change our experience of what God is like? How can we let God grow up for us? One way to begin to answer these questions is to take a developmental view of maturation.

PEOPLE GROW UP (SOMETIMES)

As infants, we humans are a dependent lot. Very few species take as long to grow out of the infancy stage as we do. For the first nine months or so, babies only know what is immediate: warmth, cold, hunger, the breast. They are one with what they feel. They *are* hunger, coldness, heat, nursing. Around the age of nine months, infants develop object permanence. They learn that things (and, more importantly, Mommy) still exist even when they are out of sight and touch. Peek-a-boo becomes possible because the baby learns that the other people aren't really gone when they hide. And so instead of crying, the baby laughs. The mind begins to expand beyond simple oneness with the moment at hand.

Eventually, as the baby becomes a small child, the mind expands even further to include the sky, imagination, language, shadows and light, thought, dreams, and the magic of the universe. My son, who couldn't have been more than three at the time, while staring out the car window one day, quietly uttered "God is everywhere," right out of the blue. The world becomes a magic place, filled with glory, terror, and mystery. Fantastic reasons for the existence of natural phenomena are created.

After magic begins the process of reasoning. As the mind grows, it is no longer content to simply experience the wonder and mystery of life. Life must begin to have order. Logic and fairness enter in. Nothing became more serious for our children than the exact division of a candy bar between them. Nothing was more incomprehensible to them than inconsistency.

As children grow older, becoming teenagers and young adults, their moral development takes them further out into the world. As boundaries expand they now enter a wider social group beyond the family. Friends, gangs, teams, fellow students, or one's musical subculture become all-important. Teenagers and young adults begin to feel as part of a group, and adopt the manner, thinking, and values of that group. Sometimes they take part in protests and social activism. The wider world of injustice, racism, and ecology become important.

The next stage usually involves a movement into individuation and the awareness of meaning and purpose. Life decisions are often made, such as marriage, parenthood, education, and vocation. In order to make these decisions, we must find out what we really think as individuals. We are led into the necessity for individual development and exploration of meaning by the very experiences which often come about at this age. We go into the workplace or get married and have a child, and suddenly find that we are having to define the meaning of fidelity, discipline, honesty, and purpose. We create a lifestyle based upon our individual values and sense of meaning. Often this sense of meaning and individual purpose is naïve and overly confident. We have not been tested yet.

Middle age brings, with the passage of time, the tests that break open the confidence and optimism of youth. We fail. People hurt us. Big problems don't go away as we get older; Alcoholism, anxiety, and divorce persist. We fall down, run up against irreconcilable paradox and realize that half our life is over. We are going to die, and it may occur sooner than we expected. We begin to wonder if maybe we won't ever fully become the people we thought we would. Cynicism is always possible during this time of life.

This middle age crisis which so many have to go through can give way, if we keep maturing, to an ability to have patience with the complexity, imperfection, diversity, and paradox of life. We gain perspective as we learn over time that we don't have to achieve what we thought we should before we die.

Eventually, a few find wisdom. They return to the simple pleasure and magic of life which many had as very small children, only now they are childlike instead of childish. Simple wisdom has been bought at a price. Knowing the complexity and disappointment of life, the wise ones find unity with all that is and happiness in whatever circumstances are at hand. They are not passive, for they have discovered their individualism and know their strength. They are content and yet fully awake and engaged.

Any model of human development has large gaping holes, including this one. Some people never make it out of the naïve group mentality of those teenage and early adult years, even though they grow old. They never find their individuality and certainly never accept paradox and diversity. Some are broken by the crises of middle age, never accepting their imperfection, or never learning patience. Crushed and angry, they take it out on others. Many never find wisdom. Others, on the other hand, learn life's lessons only too early. They pass through middle age before they are out of their teens. Some even find the peace of contentment as young adults. But while this brief account of human development does not describe everyone, it does paint a common picture. Many of us move through a process of growing up that resembles this model.

SPIRITUAL PILGRIMAGE

One of the remarkable things about the Bible is that it chronicles the social, moral, and spiritual pilgrimage of a people through history. There are some striking parallels between the spiritual development of the people of Israel and individual human development as I have briefly sketched it. Furthermore, we can see similarities between our own spiritual development and the historical journey of Israel. (For the portion of the discussion that follows, which is concerned with spiritual development, I am indebted to James Fowler, for his book *Stages of Faith*.)

The oldest writings of the Bible, collected in Genesis and Exodus, are representative of a young community of people.

Israel told these stories for generations long before they were written down, and they closely resemble many stories from other primitive cultures. In fact, some of them seem to have been borrowed and adapted from ancient Canaanite mythology. They were written not as historical descriptions of what happened but were rather told and retold over the centuries as a way of teaching some of the mysteries of God, nature, and humanity.

The first stories of the Bible, fashioned out of the experiences of a primitive tribe of people, are like the world of the preschooler. Magic, mystery, and wondrous events abound, one after the other. The heavens and the earth are created out of a formless void by the powerful, simple utterance of God. Humans are crafted by the Creator's hands out of the earth. A flood covers the earth and an ark contains all that is left of the animal kingdom. A woman is turned into a pillar of salt. A man wrestles with an angel all night. A bush burns but is not consumed as a voice emerges from it. Moses has a magic staff that changes into a serpent, turns water into blood, creates swarms of frogs, gnats, and flies, finally controlling the seas so that the Israelites pass safely and the Egyptians are drowned. Bread falls from the sky and water flows from a rock.

This is the language and imagery of magic. Israel, at the time in which these stories were told, was in its preschool age, developmentally speaking. The world was full of mystery and God acted in dramatic, amazing ways. This is the place where little children are naturally, and is sometimes a stage in the spiritual development of adults as well. This point of view is important. We need to be in touch with the wonder of a life in which miracles really do happen and not everything can be explained by logic.

However, if one remains here and seizes upon religious magic as a kind of end in itself, problems arise. For instance, some of those within pentecostal and charismatic Christianity remain stuck in this exciting stage of magic and power. Not all

within these traditions do, but some will, like a child, emphasize the mighty acts of God or the nefarious works of Satan and
his demons—speaking in mysterious tongues, rolling on the
floor in ecstacy, and being "slain in the spirit." Coincidences
are seen as amazing proof of God's powerful guiding hand and
ill fortune as a sign of the devil's strength and presence. Some
adults remain in this relatively immature stage of spiritual development all of their life.

The "older childhood" stage of Israel's growth was the beginning of the Law. Their world expanded beyond the simple
wonder of creation and deliverance, and moved into the first
phase of moral discernment. The nation of Israel began to
order their world through legislation of right and wrong. Their
initial Ten Commandments soon expanded to hundreds of or-
dinances governing every single aspect of their lives. Like children who want to know exactly what their limits are and what
they can and cannot do, Israel lived in the world of the Law.
One's worth and standing with God was measured by one's
faithfulness to its dictates.

This is often the next phase of spiritual development for
us as well. Moving out of the wonder and awareness of the
power of God, we get interested in the boundaries. What is the
right and proper way to live? What does God require of us?
How can we be faithful? While this is a useful phase, some become and remain preoccupied with religious right and
wrong—especially wrong. Dancing and gambling are bad. So
are all forms of sexual activity outside of marriage. Divorce,
even in the case of physical abuse, is wrong. Abortion, even in
the case of rape, is evil. A woman should obey her husband.
Everyone should accept Jesus in a certain way and go to
church regularly. Sins are sought out, identified, and hunted
down with great relish. The world is caught in a war of light
against darkness, and woe to those who dwell even in the shadows. God metes out punishment and reward. There is little or

no mercy. The church has been the interpreter and intermediary of this stern legalism. In its more extreme forms, it has resulted in violence against heretics and practitioners of "evils" such as abortion. Legalism may just be a stage, but those who remain for very long, even in the milder forms of legalism, are still children in the faith, addicted to an immature and imaginary security.

After the establishment of the Law, Israel, like a teenager, moved into the stage of the tribe. They solidified their formation as a people, with definite customs and ways, set apart from and often battling those who were not a part of the Jewish tribe. This tribe, now the Chosen People, conquered the Canaanites who lived there and occupied what they called the Promised Land. The Law now became a way of binding the people together.

For contemporary religious seekers, primitive legalism often gives way to a consciousness of the group and its way of life. The system of the church, with its sacraments, holy days, fasts, and festivals becomes an all-enclosed and lifegiving world view. One belongs to a group and takes on its rules of life. In being a part of a religious tribe, there is a sense of belonging, submission to a tradition that is older and wiser than oneself, and security. While this too is a useful stage in faith development, the sense of belonging can take on other more destructive qualities for those who do not move beyond it. Everything becomes so important within the system that life itself outside the system may be forgotten. These people develop an attachment that becomes self-serving; they can poison a community with tunnel vision and smug exclusivism.

Like young adults, Israel then moved into social awareness. Their sense of right and wrong moved outward from the individual and the tribe to their society. Prophets spoke of justice for outsiders and peacemaking between nations. They preached to their leaders who often did not listen, lost as they were in greed, militarism, and corruption. These prophets

risked and often lost their lives in their passion for God's justice. The last of these great prophets in Judaism before Christ
was John the Baptist, but many came before him who called
upon the nation to be a holy and compassionate people. The
Law now evolved into the demand for national righteousness.

   This is the beginning of spiritual maturity, when a person
has journeyed past magic, legalism, and tribalism, and begins
to develop a social consciousness that is a part of her faith life.
Issues of peace and economic justice, environmentalism, and
racism are more than secular, social issues: they are some of
the very places where we are called to live out our faith. They
are arenas where love and compassion arise out of prayer and
commitment to God. For the Christian who sees this social
gospel, God is the source of both mercy and justice, calling followers to live the same way. However, in its less mature and
stagnant manifestations, Christian activism can display a naïve
utopianism or an arrogant self-righteousness that easily evolves
into cynicism. When this happens, religious activism can become an anxious, angry place.

   The people of Israel, in the middle age of their maturity,
developed what is known now as the Wisdom tradition. At this
time the Psalms and Proverbs were collected and edited, and
the books of Job, Ecclesiastes, and the Song of Solomon were
written. In these writings we find what is really a midlife crisis.
After the devastating experience of military defeat and subse-
quent exile to Babylon, they began to question their basic assumptions. Over and over God is questioned: Where are you,
and why don't you do something about our misery? The
ironies of life are apparent, and the sophisticate knows that perhaps God doesn't always reward the just and punish the
wicked. Cynically, some begin to believe that perhaps social
justice is not as important as enjoying the pleasures of life. The
clarity of right and wrong has broken down, and paradox is a
part of their world view. Having been knocked around a bit,

Israel begins to get a little less certain, a little more agnostic about some aspects concerning God. But failure and exile have also brought a kind of humility and breadth of thought.

Those who are in this place spiritually are not necessarily more mature than those in the tradition of the social gospel. But at least here it is more difficult to be self-righteous and certain about what constitutes the justice and mercy of God. The seeker who has been broken open spiritually has no choice but to be a little more agnostic. This can be a good thing, because while faith is simple, it is not simplistic. But passion may diminish, and cynicism is always a danger. The sophisticated (and often educated) Christian of this kind is at times so worldly about the faith that there is little, if any, faith left.

Israel passed into a new level of spiritual development with Jesus Christ and his followers. I am not saying that Christians are more spiritually mature than Jews, for there are no doubt many Jews who have passed into this next stage of spiritual development, and most Christians have not. It's just that my understanding of Jewish spirituality is limited to the scriptures, by and large, and the Christian scriptures begin chronologically where the Hebrew ones leave off.

Having long moved beyond primitive magic and simple legalism, not content with tribal religion, social prophecy, or even sophisticated wisdom, Jesus and his followers now come from a very different place. Like a child, the old wise ones, or true contemplatives, Jesus lived in wonder, seeing the presence of God in all. His was a vision of unity of all the world's people, and their essential oneness with God as well. Jesus awakened some and bewildered others with his profound knowledge of the human heart. Refreshingly, he pointed to the presence of God outside of religion, in the midst of life, in the most unlikely people and situations. A wise master, Jesus turned his followers inside out as he moved them from reliance upon conventional wisdom and human effort to a radical conversion of the heart. Enlightened by this conversion, they now found themselves living out of the fresh springs of a direct experience with God.

This spiritual enlightenment is the fullest expression of faith. Those who persist in their practice find this awakened peace "which is beyond all understanding," as Paul described it. Having passed through spiritual death to new life, the unity of all in God is a known reality. A quiet but energetic wisdom characterizes those who have grown into this way of being. Having been around the block a few times, they are not naïve, but they are simple. These contemplatives also recognize their soulmates in other traditions, as did Thomas Merton in his pilgrimage to Buddhist Asia. This is because they have passed beyond the confines of religion as a closed system to an open awareness of God-in-life. Their religion has been broken open and set free.

Just as any model of human development has big holes in it, so must this model of the spiritual growth of both Israel and individual seekers. People do not often move neatly through predictable stages of faith and it is not my intention to suggest that they do. We all have an individual faith history that uniquely winds through and combines some of these stages described, and others as well. However, there does exist within the broad spectrum of religion all of these primitive and more mature expressions of faith. It is possible to mature spiritually, and this growth is characterized, I believe, by movement toward the contemplative, unitive experience. But we don't begin in this place. And we usually have some resistance to letting God grow up. What is often required is a basic shift of who we think God is, or *how* God is.

GOD GROWS UP

We have grown accustomed to knowing and talking about God as if God were a person: a person who is much like us, only bigger, better, wiser, more loving, and powerful. We speak of God as having plans like we do. God thinks, speaks, acts, looks on our situation, and decides what to do next. God is a being, like us. As we imagine ourselves to be a kind of thing with a fixed personality living within the confines of a physical body, we imagine God to be a kind of fixed thing as well. And so as separate beings, we think that we have or don't have a relation-ship with God, that it is "good" or "bad." We relate from over here, this "I," to God over there, just as we do in our relations with other people. Our theology, prayer, and awareness of God all come out of this way of seeing God. We ask God to do things. We think that we are together only when we are consciously paying attention to God. We wonder what God thinks of us.

This experience and expression of God has been useful. In anthropomorphizing God, we enable our spiritual life to be per-sonal, emotional, and dynamic. Making God into a person has been a vehicle for our spiritual practice, and that practice has been at times very effective. This relationship does much good for many; it results in love, personal growth, action on behalf of those who suffer, recovery from abusive addictions and behav-iors, and a prayerful awareness of God in the moment. But this view of God is quickly wearing out its usefulness for many.

How can modern, contemplative people "relate to" God as a being apart from us, after we have come to know, perhaps through meditation, the fact of our unity with all that is? How can we think dualistically about God, ourselves, and life, after we have experienced being awake to and at one with, even for a moment, the sacredness of an ordinary moment? Taking in our breath, we feel God's life in us, a life that permeates the whole world. How can we "have a relationship" with what we have come to know as the deepest level of our own being, of all being?

Modern physics has given us much to think about. The universe, down to the smallest particle, seems driven by a uni-tive energy source. All is change and motion; nothing is fixed and solid, not even our bodies. All is in a process of dying and being reborn. Creation and destruction are continually happening, from subatomic to biological to universal levels. Our subjective consciousness, our thought and awareness, measurably affects physical changes in seemingly separate entities. All that is, seen and unseen, is sustained, connected, and continually recreated by some mysterious force.

As a result of our exposure to contemplative awareness in meditation, physics, and more, God is beginning to grow up for us. Perhaps now we can let go of the security of keeping God as a thing for ourselves, as a being. Perhaps now we can come to know God simply as *Being* itself. Perhaps we can allow God to be the creative and dynamic energy within us and throughout the universe, of life and love. Being is what we experience when we know our oneness in the ordinary moment. Being is what we experience, even without being conscious of it, in the simple act of taking a breath, creating and destroying cells, thinking, and acting.

Some have called this awareness of God in all of life panentheism. This is to distinguish it from pantheism, which says that God *is* a tree, God *is* the earth, I *am* God. Panentheism recognizes the presence of God in the tree, in the earth, in the self. But it also knows that we humans can act in ways that are contrary to that presence within, and that in this sense there is also separation. Panentheism also knows that this presence of God is not limited to the form in which it is present. God transcends form, and will continue to exist even if all form is destroyed. But whether it is called panentheism or contemplation, it is seeing God not as a being who acts upon life, but as Being itself that is acting through life.

If God is Being, then union with God is not something to be achieved; it is a fact of life. If God is Being, then our efforts in prayer are not directed toward having a dialogue between two beings; our efforts are to open ourselves to what is, and what can be realized in us, with awareness. If God is Being, then when we sin we have not offended a divine person; we have simply tried to act in a way that is contrary to Being, to the way things are. Sin doesn't work and it painfully disrupts life. If God is Being, then when we love we are not simply pleasing or being obedient to a divine person; we are moving with, rather than against, the Being of all life. Love is what works and it is how things are.

For contemplatives, what is this God like, who is Being itself? On the one hand, this is a silly question and it may be arrogant to try to answer it. On the other hand, while we may not be able to describe God, we can certainly try to describe our experience of God. I can only speak for myself, and describe what I know; this can only be done by looking at the practice of open-awareness contemplative prayer, where my experience of God is concentrated. By looking at what prayer is like, we see what God is like for us.

In meditative prayer as I know it, the purpose is not to try to "get to God," to get God to do something, to figure something out, to become a better person, or to have a wonderful experience of what we think holiness is. The purpose is to become aware of life as it truly is for us at any moment and to learn to embrace it. By doing so, we begin to see our own fears and attachments, as well as the inherent holiness of life as it already is. Then when action and change are called for, we are more likely to act clearly and lovingly, instead of trying to manipulate the world out of our fears and attachments in order to meet our idea of the way things ought to be.

In this "open-awareness contemplation," we sit in silence for lengthy periods. Staying open to whatever comes up, and holding it before God in an act of simple offering, we are open to the presence of God in all. Whatever we find our mind or emotions doing in this silence—analyzing, worrying, fantasizing, planning—we watch it and hold it before God. Sitting through all of it, knowing we are in God and God is in us, we allow it to be. We watch what we generate over and over in the vain attempt to control our life, to avoid pain, and to gain what we want. Over time we begin to see the patterns, the ways in which we try to control, and thereby separate ourselves from life, from others, from God, from being alive in the moment. We discover how, in the attempt to avoid life's suffering we re-create, again and again, the deeper suffering of separation. These patterns are, over time, gradually robbed of their power as we reveal them to the light of truth. Thus we offer our lives as they really are to God, and God offers transforming grace to us.

This kind of prayer becomes a microcosm of our life. It is a concentrated arena where our issues can be revealed. It is a place where change is affected in a profound and focused way, and this in turn changes our life. For if we can simply accept where we are in a moment of prayer, we can begin to accept all of life. Accepting whatever life brings us, we affirm its essential goodness, its *Godness*. No matter what is going on in our active little minds, no matter what is going on (positively or negatively) in the drama of our life, we begin to trust that God is in it. As such, life as it really exists is to be tasted, chewed, and digested rather than avoided, manipulated, or grasped. We pay attention to the fullness of what is, rather than trying to change what is into some kind of other, imagined fullness. We learn to have an active curiosity about the details of life, because the details are all we have, in the end. It is very hard work, but being curious leads to being appreciative or reverent in all circumstances. We see things as they are, rather than wishing them to be something different, and we discover our patterns of resistance and manipulation that block us from love, from God.

We begin to be in less of a hurry. If this moment is where God is to be known and appreciated, we start to see God in this very ordinary (or even unpleasant) moment, and cease the effort to rush to some other, imagined place of "holiness." Life becomes less worrisome, because we discover that whatever is worrying us is usually, in fact, the very next arena of God's presence and new life as we open to it. We become a little lighter, more ready to see the humor in situations. We are a bit more playful, because we are no longer playing the deadly, serious game of making sure that things go our way. When we are confronted with our limits, weaknesses, stupidity, and sin we needn't be threatened, defensive, or ashamed. Embracing even these moments in our curiosity and appreciation for all of life, we learn and move more swiftly through them, trusting God's presence to transform us through these limitations.

Selfless love becomes possible. Rather than seeing people as experiences that we want to either avoid or cling to, we can see them as they are, with appreciation. When we stop our self-centered emotional fleeing and grasping, we can enjoy who others are. Whether they are attractive or repellant, angry or sweet, we can simply see them as they are, with curiosity and even reverence. We can experience their energy without judgment, not having to either run away from it or absorb it. God can then be seen in the eyes of everyone. When we allow others this kind of space to be themselves, where they are in that moment, without rejecting or grasping on to them, others have a chance to know the unconditional acceptance of God's love through us.

With contemplative practice and awareness, we gradually become more like this. We become more reverent and relaxed. We become lighter and more playful. We lose more of our fear and useless, busy striving. We are more loving. This is a description of our own spiritual awareness. But because it is an experience of God, it is also a description of God: God *is* reverence, peace, light, playfulness, openness, renewal, freedom, happiness, truth, courage, and love. These are the qualities of God which we can know. The presence of these qualities, the presence of this God, awakens us. When we worship God, we are worshiping this presence because it transforms us into the person that we have been created to be. We seek and love this presence, because it is the true nature of everything in the universe, seen and unseen. We want to become like it.

This nature of God is universal. No one religion owns it, and it is available in myriad forms. But underneath its forms, its character is consistent. God's nature is love, freedom, renewal, and truth. God is always like this, no matter in what form God is revealed. God is not just what we subjectively make God up to be. The nature of God has an objective quality, character, or personality about it. We can say that this is what God is like.

This fact was forcefully brought home to me some years ago in a workshop when we were asked to recall a transformative experience of God, a time when we knew God's presence to be real. We were to pay close attention to its quality. What was it like for us, what was the effect of it upon our emotions, our body, our thinking? We were then to return as a group and describe our experiences to one another.

This was a diverse group of people. Ranging in age from the early thirties to the late seventies, the thirty of us also represented the spectrum of theological points of view. Nearly every Christian denomination was there, and a few non-Christians as well. When we came back together an amazing thing happened. The experiences of God we described were all different in form, and yet they were all the same in character.

One charismatic woman recalled speaking in tongues. A Presbyterian minister of a prosperous congregation described being pronounced dead of a heart attack and leaving his body before coming back. Another person talked about water-skiing on LSD twenty-five years ago. Someone else spoke of their recovery from addiction to alcohol. A woman told us of giving birth to her first child. A man recalled a simple moment of walking down the street and waking up to something that has never left him. All of the circumstances were different, as were the theological interpretations of the events.

But they were all the same. When recalling the character of these events, we were all describing the same thing: peace in what were not necessarily peaceful circumstances; light, the naked truth, quiet but powerful alertness, calm and utter trust in the moment, grateful wonder in the details of what was at hand, stillness within action, a radical and very real death and rebirth, freedom from fear, oneness with all that is, decisive clarity and unconditional love. Describing our experiences of God, we were describing the nature of God. This is what God is like. This is whom we seek in prayer and worship. This is all that matters. This is what all humans can become. It is our true nature. This is the character of God beneath all forms of religion and non-religion.

If you go beneath the form of religious symbol, practice, and theology, and you manage to get to the actual experience that is being communicated through these forms, this character is always what you will find. Sufis dance to awaken themselves to this God-experience. Native Americans sit all night in the intensity of a sweat lodge and emerge, renewed by it. Christians eat and drink this quality of life through the presence of Christ in the Eucharist. Addicts die to their attachment and are reborn by the vitality of God-in-life. And as they go through these things, beneath what they are calling it and how they conceptualize it, they are all having the same experience of the one God.

The tradition other than Christianity with which I am most familiar is Zen Buddhism. Here is an agnostic tradition, which seemingly is not interested in the existence or nonexistence of God. But if you listen deeply to the experience toward which Buddhism points, you will hear what we call God. If you look beneath the practice of Buddhism to what is described as the fruit of practice, you will see what we call God, the same fruit of our practice as Christians.

The fruit of Buddhist practice is "no-self," or put in a positive way, the attainment of Buddha-nature. This nature lies beneath all individual human personalities, in fact beneath the forms of all sentient beings, and has a definite character about it. It is a dying to aversion and desire, just letting that endless cycle die through ruthless attention to it. In dying to our usual way of living life—seeking pleasure and avoiding pain, building up our personality—there is a rebirth which takes place. We begin to live out of a source of true life which is not our own. The "I" does not exist anymore; we live instead out of a wellspring that is available to all. It is not a matter of our understanding. It is the spontaneous, fresh reality of life itself that empowers us. It is the true nature of our being, and it is who and what all sentient beings are, beneath the illusion of the individual self.

This wellspring is called various things: Big Mind, Buddha-nature, Nirvana, True Nature, Enlightenment. We become an empty vessel for the expression of this life flowing through us, and it is so consistent in its character that its authenticity is recognizable by those who know it. That is why Zen masters are able to discern whether one has passed a *koan* or has grown in the awakened life. This is how dharma heirs are found and how the lineage of the teaching continues. The objective character of this wellspring that flows through us is peace, alertness, and appreciation for the moment. It is a sense of humor and freedom. It is a willingness to stand gratefully under the judgment of the naked truth. It is compassion for all living beings.

This sure sounds like God to me. Paul spoke of no-self when he said, "I have been crucified with Christ; and it is no longer I who live but it is Christ who lives in me" (Gal. 2:19b–20a). He was describing our true nature in which all of us already dwell when he said, "In [God] we live and move and have our being" (Acts 17:28). And he spoke of the enlightenment which is beyond dualistic reason and effort when he said that "the peace of God which surpasses all understanding will guard your hearts and your minds in Christ Jesus" (Phil. 4:7).

I believe that this reality, which contemplative Christians (including Paul) have always known, is the experience of mature seekers everywhere. Perhaps the church can begin to proclaim through its mainstream what it has always known on the edges of its tradition. I also believe that the world is finally ready for this vision of God. God knows the world needs it.

WHAT IS THE WORLD COMING TO?

*I*n some ways the world is getting worse. Materialism, once confined largely to the West, is sweeping even third world countries as megacorporations, home satellite dishes, and the media reach into the most remote regions of the world. Indifference to and outright oppression of the poor, along with shortsighted economic policies, continue unabated and threaten ecological and social stability. Overpopulation brings crime, pollution, and widespread disease. We may have graduated beyond world wars, but regional hatreds erupt constantly. It often feels as if we are all on the edge of disaster.

On the other hand, ours is a time of great awareness. Participation in traditional religion may be lower than it has been in the past, but astounding numbers of people meditate, seek the help of a "higher power," or find honesty and fulfillment through the help of therapy. Many of those millions of us who took psychedelic drugs in the 1960's were opened up to a spiritual orientation in a way that will never be closed again. More and more people are aware that the solution to the big problems of the world can only be found through a spiritual conversion of humanity's heart. People are beginning to pay very close attention to the ecological unity of all living beings on this one planet. From space, we have seen the earth as a single, integrated whole and that has changed our consciousness. The computer networks have linked people everywhere with an immediacy never before possible. The Western world has met the

East, and the North the South. We are all affected by this rich interchange of humanity.

We have all been forced to encounter, far more than ever before, diversity in our culture: ethnic, sexual and political. Many are much more aware of the economic interdependence of haves and have-nots, knowing that the welfare of the individual is inseparable from the welfare of all. In some ways, the closed systems of many "isms" have broken open. One earth, one people, one economy, one God, one spiritual journey, one life—all expressed in an incredible profusion of diversity. This can be a contemplative, unitive time for those with eyes to see it.

Will we choose to mature? Thomas Berry, in his visionary *Dream of the Earth*, poignantly reveals the magnitude of our choice. He describes the earth as one living organism, which in its historical evolution has produced out of itself human life. Humanity is only one of the many species to bloom out of the earth. And while humanity is not superior, it is different from other species in one important way. We have self-consciousness, and with it, a wondrous and terrible power to create and to destroy. We can discover penicillin and we can melt holes in the atmosphere. We express ourselves uniquely, through beautiful forms: art, science, religion, literature, and love. We also express ourselves uniquely through hatred and mindless greed. In a very real sense, the earth has grown a mind, and we are that mind. In evolving itself into this particular form, the earth has taken a huge risk. This mind, this self-consciousness of the earth may destroy itself and much of the rest of the earth, at least temporarily. But the potential for gain is at least as great. We may evolve further into a more wise and skilled presence on the planet, caring mindfully not only for ourselves but also for the rest of the earth.

The passing of millennia has always been a time of both crisis and opportunity for the world. It is not just symbolic. There is something substantial for us in crossing these thresholds.

Something changes. As we rapidly approach the year 2,000, humanity will arrive at a new crossroads. We may choose immature short-sightedness and remain selfishly stuck, sealing our own fate with disastrous consequences. We may also begin to grow up. More of us may choose the path of wisdom and maturity, utilizing our newfound sensitivity to unity within diversity. I do not believe that utopia is possible in this world, but I do believe we can cooperate more in the effort to grow beyond war, clean up our environment, provide health care, feed ourselves, and educate our children. This cooperation is especially possible now, since for the first time in history we really know our common physical and spiritual identity and destiny.

And so we stand at the crossroads. We will, no doubt, choose some mixture of both possibilities. Suffering and greed will never be eliminated. But we may grow up a bit. Until now we have, as a species, acted like spoiled children or myopic adolescents. Perhaps we can grow into mature adulthood. We may grow up because we have become aware of the consequences of not growing up. We may also grow up because of a more unitive spirituality and wisdom that some know.

Like Israel, or the individual spiritual seeker, humanity's journey has brought us forward to the point of potential awareness. Like the maturing seeker, we have the opportunity to leave both legalism and tribalism behind. Law and order, or the protection and defense of our own various groups will not solve the problems of this age. If we mature, it will also be because we, like the maturing seeker, grow beyond the thinking that social consciousness and strenuous efforts toward justice will be enough. We must also grow beyond worldly wisdom, beyond the increased knowledge and information of modern sophistication. We need further maturation into the contemplative spirit of wisdom. We need to wake up. We need reverence and mutual respect. We need a mindful, open awareness. It is now a matter of survival, and the church can help.

WILL THE CHURCH FOLLOW AND LEAD?

Obviously, this is not the only time in history that a cultural shift in perspective has happened. And when society shifts, the church follows, pushing the shift along even further with its attention to the human spirit. Social and ecclesiastical, even theological, histories are completely intertwined. The Roman Empire—with its enforced peace and safety for travelers, combined with the common language of Greek—enabled the initial spread of Christianity in the first few centuries. Christian theology then began to flower in the hothouse atmosphere of "secular" philosophical debate during the same period. Paradoxically, the giant step backwards taken by society during the chaos of the Dark Ages provided the needed atmosphere for the rise of monastic orders, with their tremendous influence upon the feudal system. The opening up of culture and education in the High Middle Ages produced yet another flowering of radical new theologians, some thought to be heretics at the time, St. Thomas Aquinas among them. The development of world exploration, military, and economic expansion brought further intellectual expansion, paving the way for even more radical debate about faith and the institutional church, giving way to the revolution which was the Reformation. The industrial age, in its exploitation of workers and mechanization of life, sowed the seeds for the social gospel.

To the social changes wrought in the latter part of the twentieth century, the church can respond again. By and large, the Christian church has not, to put it mildly, been terribly swift to respond to societal shifts. Ecclesiastical trials of heretics have frequently marked the church's resistance. All too often in times of tremendous change the church manifests itself as a closed system, clinging desperately to a theology that has outgrown its usefulness. It forgets that theology about God is not God. Theology always has and always will develop and even change as a people's awareness of God develops and changes. Unfortunately, the church often clutches its truth as if it were a thing, a possession to protect. In dangerous times, the grip grows tighter. Our age of transition is no different from other ones in this respect. The church, in certain quarters, is manifesting all the same signs of clinging and rigidity. But as the *I Ching* reminds us, dangerous times are also times of great opportunity. The window is now open for a breakthrough in the development of the church.

If Christianity is to be a part of the needed maturation for our common human life on this earth, it must be open to a different way of experiencing, and then talking about, God. It is time. The world is becoming more globally conscious, psychologically sophisticated, and awake to the unity of diverse forms of spiritual awareness in everyday life. So must we become in our religious life. The church must now reclaim, grow into, and offer to the world its centuries-old minority view, the contemplative way. If we do not make this shift in both awareness and expression, the church will die. The world is even now moving past the church. People are finding their spiritual needs met in other, more mature places. The church will die if it does not evolve in this critical time of growth for humankind.

The contemplative vision of God which is so needed by the world at this time is nothing new in Christianity. Jesus himself knew his oneness with God and called us to the same realization. His last prayer to God before his arrest, trial, and death was that "they may be one; even as you are in me and I am in you, may they also be in us" (John 17:21). The early desert fathers and mothers were early contemplatives, seeking to rid themselves of all images and preconceptions of God, relying instead upon a naked experience of God in the moment. Many of the collected accounts of these radical hermits are strikingly similar to Zen stories, marked by humor and uncompromising zeal. In one, a monk is told by his spiritual father in

God to throw away his Bible because he has become attached to its words. His ideas and images of God were getting in the way of the living God.

The early Christian theologian Origen taught that in Christ, God became human so that humans could become God. Many of his contemporaries spoke of the process of "divinization" or "deification" that happens to Christians by the action of grace. The medieval mystic Meister Eckhart narrowly escaped excommunication by saying that "the eye with which we see ourselves is the same eye with which God sees us," among other things. Later, St. John of the Cross described in great detail the maturation of the pilgrim who passes from relating to God as a being, through a dark night of loss, and finally to union with the God who is beyond all form and thought. The eighteenth-century Jesuit Jean-Pierre de Cassaude advised his spiritual directees to put their trust in the moment at hand, because in "the sacrament of the present moment" God is revealed in what is. The mid-twentieth-century theologian Paul Tillich taught us to think of God as "the ground of our being." In our own time, Thomas Merton was a mature voice who became simpler and clearer over his years, until finally transcending religious boundaries. The God he knew in prayer was the same experience that Buddhists describe in their enlightenment.

This contemplative tradition of the church has, perhaps, finally found its age. The world may finally be ready for a vision of God that helps us to move into reverence, unity in diversity, compassion, and respect for the spiritual nature of all life. It is time for us in the church to openly celebrate our rich tradition of the unitive vision of God. It is time for us to join those of other traditions, set the gospel free and open our religion out into life. It is time to get out of the way and let God grow up for the church, even as God is growing up for the world. For God blows through our boundaries like the wind.

4

Becoming Who We Are

I will not live an unlived life.
I will not live in fear
of falling or catching fire.
I choose to inhabit my days.
— *The Gift*, D. Markova

UNION AND SEPARATION

When God grows up for us, a different kind of relationship—if it can be called a relationship—is called for. No longer are we two separate beings who interact across the distance that we imagine to lie between beings. We are now related to God as the body is to the breath. Essentially, we are one.

No one I know, however, lives all the time in full awareness of this union with God which is our true nature. We are all, to one degree or another, separated from experiencing what is. We know our union at times, and we don't know it at others. For our recognition of it to grow, we must practice. In order to practice this kind of faith in a grown-up God, we must learn to be comfortable within the paradox of our human/divine condition.

In an absolute sense, God simply is. All is love and the pure energy of God's goodness. We live right now in eternity, at one with Being and all other beings. There is no separation.

This is what Buddhists mean when they say that we are already enlightened. There is no "where" to get to other than where we are right now. This is what baptism celebrates, in part: that we are one with God our Creator. This is what the Eucharist also celebrates, in part: that we are already one with Christ. We eat the body of Christ and as the church we are the Body of Christ. We are what we eat.

On the other hand, we are, in a relative sense, separated. We are distracted and we sin. We fear and grasp after illusions. We hate rather than love and help perpetuate institutionalized economic greed, indifference, and injustice. Even though we are already enlightened with the light of God, we do not know it. It must be realized, made real. Dualism is an illusion, but we live in duality. *Samsara*, the world of illusion, must be dealt with in order to get beyond it. We cannot simply skip past it. We are too caught up in it. So paradoxically, we must practice in order to achieve what we already have. This is also what Baptism is about: dedication to a life of practicing the Christian way so that we may realize our birthright. This is what the Eucharist is about as well: we offer our lives to God in the path of Jesus, asking for the grace to become what we already are.

This paradox of unity and separation is the subject of the first story about humankind in the Bible. Adam and Eve dwell in paradise, naked and unashamed, possessing everything they need. This is the original human state. Ultimately, we live peaceably with God. However, because they are temporal, imperfect humans like us, Adam and Eve seek to grasp control for themselves. Simple unity is not enough. They taste the forbidden fruit of the tree of the knowledge of good and evil. They want to know good and evil, to be the ones who distinguish, control, and determine. Stepping out of trust in what is, they want the power to judge and go looking for something else on their own. Now they have created separation from God.

The myth of Adam and Eve is the most basic reality of human existence. It is our story. Adam, after all, means "humanity" or "of the earth." The Garden of Eden, and what takes place there, is the starting point for all of us. Like Adam and Eve we are, paradoxically, one with God and separated from God. So in an eternal sense, God is pure Being who is everpresent; ultimately, we needn't ask for anything; salvation is not something to be achieved—it is our home. Yet we are separated from God in our awareness and we have therefore created a broken world, in which we also live. We need help; we need salvation. And so our image of God must include both Being, with whom we are already one, and Savior, who gives us the grace to realize what we are created to be. This is not an easy paradox, and we should not be too quick to resolve it by falling comfortably to one side of the problem or the other.

Because this paradox is difficult, we must find a way of working with it. That way is prayer. Working with our union with and separation from Being brings us into a different kind of prayer.

CONTEMPLATIVE PRAYER[1]

*I*t's fine to say that our relationship with God is like the relationship of the body to the breath. But how do we pray, how do we work with this kind of relationship when we are also separated from God in our awareness? Can we really just "be" in God? A Russian Orthodox story tells of a priest who comes across a man praying in the church again and again, simply sitting in silence with a smile on his face. Finally the priest's curiosity gets the better of him and he asks the man "What are

---

1. For detailed instructions on the practice of Contemplative Prayer, see the Appendix.

you doing?" The man responds "I look at God and God looks
at me and we are happy."

Now I don't know about you, but as nice as this sounds,
it's just not the way it is when I sit in silence. Most of the time
I'm not looking at God; I'm looking at a dense tangle of
thoughts, emotions, worries, and fantasies. Most of the time
I'm not happy; I'm wanting to get up and do something else.
To sit in silent contemplation, in conscious union with the
source of our being, is very hard.

I used to think that if I just tried harder, I'd be able to; if I
learned and practiced the right technique, I'd move out of distraction into open awareness. I laid this expectation on myself
for fifteen years. In fact, most forms of prayer and meditation,
Christian and non-Christian, begin with this expectation: that
we should learn to gently push aside distractions and rest in
silent, open peace. Various techniques are offered in the ac-
complishment of this goal, and most of them have to do with
concentration upon some image or thought. The theory is that
over time, the object of our concentration will grow as our distractions fall away, and we will become more and more filled
with peace and less and less distracted. Then the spiritual state
will seep, by osmosis, into the rest of our life.

This never worked for me. To be honest, I must say that I
never became significantly less distracted. Even St. Teresa of
Avila said that "fifteen minutes of prayer is fourteen minutes of
distraction." I know that concentrated practice does, for some,
result in a greater peace, but I wonder about what is really
being accomplished. The result may be that the meditators are
simply growing in their ability to concentrate on and build up
a peaceful and empty feeling, and thereby conditioning themselves with this state, so that it is more accessible when they
choose to call upon it. But what happens to our ambition, fear,
hatred, attachment, and all the other things that motivate us
when we are not calling up our peaceful, empty state? These

forces are just as powerful as ever, and they still run our lives when we are not meditating. In concentrative meditation, we may just be applying a band-aid to the symptom, rather than addressing the root cause.

What has been helpful to me is a practice of getting to the root cause of our separation from God, from being alive in the moment. To do this, we allow the "distractions" in. Instead of narrowing our concentration on something, we take a stance of wide-open awareness. In open awareness, we watch what is actually going on in our minds, in our emotions, and in our bodies. This is, after all, really being present to what is, in fact, there. Most of us think that being present is appreciating the world around us through our senses (listening, seeing, smelling), and not thinking or worrying. But if we are thinking or worrying, then being present is being present to that, rather than trying to be present to some imagined, wished-for state of sensory awareness.

And so sitting in open awareness, we watch what we are doing, what we are generating in order to control and separate ourselves from the moment. We discover that most of the time we are maneuvering around to try to manipulate reality: by thinking controlling thoughts, we imagine ourselves in control; by thinking self-critical thoughts, we keep ourselves in a familiar, locked state of homeostasis; by imagining conflict and disaster, we hope to be able to avoid it; by generating excitement about what we'll get done, we feed the hope of getting what we want.

Watching what we are doing on a habitual basis is very useful, because by so doing we come to understand the very forces that prevent us from being empty and at peace in God. Over time, the repeated types of distraction we use become clearer to us as patterns of separation. Rather than seeing distraction as a bad thing to be avoided, we learn to be gentle with ourselves and take a curious, neutral stance with them. "Oh, look, here I go again, trying to control my day." "Ah, yes, criticizing myself again." All we do is sit and watch, sit and pay attention to what is going on. As we come to know ourselves as we really are (rather than as we think we should be), we become more vulnerable and therefore more available to the action of God's transformative grace. For as we hold ourselves before God with awareness, we become open enough to be touched by the healing force of God's love that resides within. Through vulnerable awareness, our habitual sins (ways that we separate ourselves from God) come to light and are gradually melted away by the grace of God.

BUT IS IT PRAYER?

What is going on here? How is it prayer? What is the effect of this practice upon our lives? How is God involved in it?

When we manage to sit with attention through everything that is going on, we are doing a remarkable thing. We are breaking into the cycle of suffering and sin. To simply sit through the honesty of seeing ourselves think and feel what we do in the attempt to manipulate reality, we see our manipulations for what they are. To shed light on them is to rob them of their potency. When I was a child, lying in my dark room at night, I would sometimes imagine a small sound to be a very large monster. The lemon bush scraping against my window became a hideous, screaming creature just about to break in to my room and eat me alive. When I (or more likely, my father or mother) would turn on the light, the scraping branch would lose its imagined power.

In contemplation, we bring something very powerful (a pattern of separation) into the light and watch it shrivel. If we don't do this, it will remain in the dark, larger and more powerful than it really is. We will always be controlled by what we refuse to look at. On the other hand, if we do bring it into the light, we are actively participating in the process that Christianity calls judgment, repentance, surrender, and forgiveness. This process frees us, and makes us into the person we were created to be.

I have discovered countless times that judgment is not condemnation. Judgment is simply the truth about ourselves. Judgment is the use of the judging, or critical function, which is able to discern what is what. In contemplation we are judged by reality as we see the truth of our driving patterns of control and separation. What is revealed to us in contemplation is painfully personal, and it humbles us profoundly. We see ourselves as we are. When we are paying attention to what is revealed, we are facing God's truth of where we really are in that moment. If we listen and watch, name it, and feel its physical grip upon our bodies, we are allowing God to judge us as we stand naked before the truth.

Sitting through this, not running away from it or instantly feeling guilty and asking for it to be changed, just admitting who we are and what we are doing: this is the most honest form of repentance I know. In the New Testament, the original Greek word for repentance actually means "to turn." And so it is turning to the truth of God's judgment, taking a deep breath and saying yes, it is so. This is repentance, turning toward, rather than away from, the judgment of God.

Having been "found out," having seen ourselves as we are in the light of judgment, having turned to the truth in repentance, we then have the choice to try to willfully change ourselves or simply to surrender. When we make the choice to try to change ourselves willfully into a "better" person, we will inevitably feel frustrated and guilty, because we are actually powerless to accomplish this transformation. What we don't like about ourselves just comes back again. While making the effort to change is possible and even desirable at times, it is when we surrender that deep and lasting change actually takes place.

When we choose to surrender, we allow the sin, the separation from God, to be there, and we sit with it patiently before God (ten thousand times, if necessary), trusting that our self-offering will be received and transformed. It is a popular thing to say that in holding our sin and separation before God, we then "let go" of it, as if we could make it go away by releasing it. This is still a form of controlling effort, because letting go assumes that we make our sins go away in our act of releasing them. Again, we are led to frustration and guilt: "I thought I really let go of that one, and here it is again. I must find a way to really release it!" We are never really able to let go of our attachments and aversions; we just wear them out by acknowledging them and holding them honestly before God. To do this requires a great deal of self-denial, for the last thing we want to do is give up our control, to admit our powerlessness, to be crucified.

This is truly surrendering to God. We give up when we stop trying to change ourselves by our will-power and by our attempts to let go and be rid of things. We surrender our imagined strength, and trust instead in the goodness of God to see us through it and bring us out the other side. Eventually we must let God take over the process. Our job is to simply sit in God's presence and pay attention, over and over again, to the same aversions and attachments. Grace will take care of the rest. To take this position is real faith, for it undermines any sense of getting rid of our sin on our own. We simply can't do it. We are dependent upon grace to transform us. And so we do what we can do, which is to bring our sin to awareness, as much as possible, and hold it before the One who will take it and do with it what needs to be done.

Forgiveness is that which naturally and inevitably comes after repentance and surrender. Forgiveness is not a reward, God's end of a bargain. It is the natural consequence of turning to the truth and surrendering our power to change on our own. We experience forgiveness because we are not destroyed in the process of surrendering. God's judgment and our repentance and surrender don't kill us. After sitting through the process, we're still there, in the beauty of life's moment. After we have paid attention long enough to one of our persistent sins, we are moved through it by the grace of God and we discover the freedom of not being controlled by it. We are then graced with starting over with this moment, with all its magnificent richness. This is surely the forgiveness of God, for it frees us from sin, opening us up to new life. We are resurrected by grace.

It must be remembered that this movement from judgment to new life is not always a linear or logical one. It is not a job to be mastered. It is the mystery of God's grace working in us. We can't control it or make it happen. The practice of prayer is not a self-improvement project. We cannot cook up "holiness" by following a recipe of this process.

Growing up in the San Francisco Bay Area, I used to surf at Santa Cruz. When you surf, you spend a long time out in the ocean, watching and waiting. Along comes a wave, you think it's the one that will take you, and you turn and paddle. It peters out. You wait again. This time, the wave picks you up. What is interesting is that you must use all your effort and skill to catch it, but there is a moment in which the power of the wave takes over and carries you aloft. You can feel the life of the wave. You can feel it pick you up and take you away. But it won't take you unless you've put in the effort. Once moving with the energy of the wave, your job is to give a little direction now and then, and to stay balanced and awake.

This is like the action of God's grace. We must watch and wait, sitting in silence. We must put in our effort, with everything we've got, watching what is already there. Sometimes nothing happens. But at some point, a life that is not our own rises up within us and moves us along. We may not feel this wave of grace. We may not even know it is happening. But if we stay awake and balanced, not trying too hard but giving it a little steering when needed, we will be carried forward. We can trust this ever-present, life-giving energy of God.

Taking on a discipline of contemplative prayer brings us to the root cause of sin and suffering, to the raw place of encounter between separation from and unity with God. Through this encounter something stirs deeply within us, a stirring not of our own doing. Everything is touched by this stirring: our relationships, our sense of self, our capacity to love, and our response to what is around us. Contemplative practice changes us. It is possible, through the hard work of practice and the grace of God, to become who we are, in our true nature. Christians become more like Jesus. We all become more like God.

CAN BEING BE PERSONAL?

*I*n practicing an open awareness before Being itself, what happens to our Christian tradition of a loving God who, in a very personal way, reaches out to us and responds to our need? What becomes of God's love and forgiveness? What of God's will? What becomes of supplicatory, penitential, and intercessory prayer? Has God been reduced to the principle of healing that takes place in contemplative awareness? Is God an impersonal energy field blipping through the universe? Fears of exactly this kind are what prevent otherwise mature Christian people from growing into a contemplative faith. These fears keep highly educated people at a Sunday School level when it comes to their religion. These fears keep the church from growing up and setting the gospel free.

To say that God is either a person who loves and saves the individual or an impersonal energy field is to oversimplify the matter. It is all too often that we oversimplify paradoxical matters by driving ourselves and others to opposite extremes. But there is no reason why we can't have a paradoxical sense of

God who is both the simple fact of Being and personal too. There is no reason why we can't imagine God as being relational, active, and loving without our image degenerating into an oversimplified, anthropomorphized Big Guy in the Sky.

How do we ask for God's help, love, and salvation without compromising our contemplative experience of God? How do we seek a relationship with God without perpetuating dualism and separation?

The subtle truth for me lies in accepting God's personal nature without seeing God as a person. Universal Being and love are personal by their very nature. We look to God as the creative source of all life, as our Creator. Creation is filled with the personal, the specific. After all, people have personalities, thoughts, will, and character; where did this come from? Our Creator must as least include the personal. When we pray to a personal Being, we are praying through that aspect of God that includes personality. So if one relates to God as a person, albeit a huge and perfect person, it's not wrong. It's just that seeing God *simply* as a person is so terribly limited. For God's personal aspect is only one element of infinite Being. And yet as personal humans, some of us may need to relate to this limited aspect of our Creator.

Furthermore, God is intertwined with the specifics of our lives; Being and love are intimately involved in everything we think, feel, and do. There is an energy, a direction, and purpose to this Being. We need this energy, direction, and purpose. To ask for it is to not only affirm our desire and need for it, it is to invite this presence to be more realized within us. In doing so, we peel back another layer of our resistance to God. God is personal when we know our need.

Let's say a beloved friend is going into the hospital for heart surgery, and everyone is worried because he is really at risk. His wife, who is beside herself, asks you to pray for him. What do you do? Do you nod your head and smile condescendingly, having no intention to lower yourself to such an immature, dualistic action? Do you swallow hard, and feeling a little silly, toss off a quick prayer to the God of your childhood? "Please pay attention here and don't let him die on the operating table."

There is another alternative. Perhaps you can, in meditative prayer, hold the relationship with your friend in your consciousness. Knowing that you are in the presence of the source of life and healing, you simply hold him there. In holding him before God, you may become aware of aspects of him you don't really like, as well as your affection for him. You also become aware of how you want him to make it through the surgery. You feel this dislike, affection, and hope and let it be there. This may give way to an ability to see him as a child of God, already in union with God. Love and light are what flow between them. Holding him there, you release your prejudices and hopes without asking anything. You let him go into God.

What have you done? You have prayed for your friend. You have not tried to get God to do something—knowing that God is not a person to be convinced of anything. But you have held your desire and his need before the source of life. What happens in this interchange? Because you are intimately, biologically, and spiritually linked to your friend (as you are to all living beings), you have together peeled back another layer of resistance and come closer to realizing God. This has opened the door a bit wider for God's ever-present grace to move through and help the situation. You have been quite personal with both God and your friend. Linked together in God, you have moved him further into God. If the intention and methodology of a physicist can actually affect physical changes in molecules, surely your awareness in God can affect another's health.

God becomes personal for us when we are seeking direction in our own lives as well. We may not believe that God makes everything happen, like a celestial puppeteer: "Elizabeth has asked for guidance in her job search, so right here on the corner of Fourth Street and Candelaria, I think I'll make her crash into her future employer's car, so they'll meet." But we can seek direction from the Being of life itself who is, in our experience, very personal and specific. In praying for herself, Elizabeth can hold her need for a change before God. As she holds it there she comes to know it: her tendency to seek change for change's sake, her genuine need for more money and autonomy. As with intercessory prayer, this form of supplication does not ask God to do anything. But it acknowledges the link that exists between what we are praying about and the presence of God. This is personal, and it makes a difference. It peels back a layer of our separation. It helps Elizabeth realize, in this specific situation, that she needn't worry. It's not that, having put in her heartfelt request, she can rest assured that God has now been convinced to do something. Rather, she stops worrying because she has brought herself back to that place where she is aware of her essential security in God. She has come closer to realizing her trust in both God's and her ability to stay open to new possibilities and recognize the right thing when it comes along.

This way of being personal with God in contemplation applies to other forms of prayer as well. We confess our sins by honestly holding our brokenness before the source of wholeness. We thank God by joining with all creation in offering our sense of gratitude in silence. We seek answers by sitting with the question before the source of all wisdom and truth.

Being personal with God means being specific about our situation and then sitting with this specific reality before the source of all life. This makes a very personal connection between our concrete circumstance and God. But what about the big one in Christian theology: What about salvation? How can we understand a personal, loving God who frees us from sin without sliding inevitably back into childish images of God? How are we saved?

SALVATION

Traditionally in mainstream Christianity, salvation has often been thought of as something like this: We are separated from God by our offenses, and we owe a big debt because of them. A really big debt. Because God is just, it must be paid. The only thing that we have that could possibly pay with is our life. But because God is loving, we can't just be killed. Besides, our death wouldn't really be good enough, since we're so blemished. We'd be an impure sacrifice. So God comes up with a plan. God decides to kill his own son, Jesus, instead. He's human, therefore he can substitute for us. He's also divine, therefore he's a clean sacrifice. So God kills him, a human sacrifice to pay for our sins. Then God strikes a deal with us. If we believe all this to be so, then we get cut in on the deal and we go to heaven after we die. If we don't, we go to hell.

This is called the substitutionary theory of the atonement. It is a popular theory, but not the only one in the history of Christian theology. However, it is the one that most people think of when they think of the cross, belief, and salvation. This theory posits God as a Big Person who has values, thoughts, feelings, and actions like ours. Predictably enough, because it grew out of the ancient Jewish practice of blood sacrifice, this theory is based upon an animal sacrifice for the restoration of at-one-ment with God. It is a primitive religion indeed that relies upon human sacrifice to satisfy an angry God. The substitutionary theory of the atonement has more in common with ancient Aztec and other blood centered religions than its proponents would care to admit. In fact, this is one of the chief reasons (other than the sword) that the Spanish conquistadors and Franciscans made such rapid religious inroads into the Aztec world of Mexico. Appeasement through blood-sacrifice was a familiar myth for Mexico's indigenous people.

A contemplative approach to salvation would look very different, because it comes out of a different theology of God.

Recall the story of Adam and Eve, our story. We are one with God, essentially good, but we move inexorably into separation, greed, and fearful controlling. This is the sinful nature that we learn and take on at a very early age. It is the false self, layered on top of our true nature. We have little choice in this, because although we are created good and at one with God, we are also born into an atmosphere of brokenness. Because it is pervasive, before we even have language we are participating in it. In this sense it is what we call Original Sin, the pervasive and inescapable nature of fallen humankind.

At some point we come across someone or something like Jesus Christ. He showed the way back to union with God through compassionate openess to all, and an immediate awareness of God-in-life. He was so convinced of this union and compassion that he was faithful to it to the end. His clarity, conviction, and faithfulness, as well as his radical message, were threatening to some. Because he believed in God-in-life rather than in religion, he was a double threat. So he, like others who are a little too close to the truth, was killed. But his continuing life-in-God after death was somehow revealed. Death was unmasked as an imposter. God and love were clearly seen to be more powerful than hatred, fear, and even death.

When we look at this series of events in Jesus' life, something inside us may hum in tune with it. We know this is true about life. We know that God is more powerful than anything. We know that if we follow the same way that Jesus did, we may have to go through a kind of spiritual crucifixion of the small ego over and over, but ultimately we've nothing to fear. If we follow the way of Jesus, we may still have just as much real pain in our lives (look how his life turned out, after all), but the wider picture of God's victorious life is always pressing upon us. We move through the troubles and suffering of life with a new lightness, a grace and confidence. This faith frees us to be the person we are called to be, since the threat is gone. We are able to be whole, because we are secure in our eternal identity in God. We are saved.

Every time we remind ourselves of our eternal identity, every time we look at a crucifix or participate in the liturgies of Good Friday and Easter, we become more assured of this freedom and salvation that comes through death to the small self. When we catch ourselves in sin, separation, greed, and fear, we can remember what is real. We can remember the cross and the resurrection as touchstones. We can remember that if we, too, pass through suffering we will be renewed by the God of victorious life and love. In specific situations we trustingly allow ourselves to die so that God may resurrect us. This is faith in the cross of Jesus, which saves us from our sin and our suffering. This is salvation, because by this action we are returned to our original at-one-ment with God.

Salvation (or wholeness, if you will) comes to us from a source that is both within and beyond us: from the very nature of reality, from God. As each of us is created uniquely and personally, so this saving energy comes to each of us uniquely and personally. We all experience the passage from death to life in different ways. The manner of God's salvation which works within us is determined by what we need. Some need a Father God who speaks and acts. Contemplatives understand salvation as the energy of life's relentless goodness and truth within them. Still others see God's saving power in other people, in therapy, and recovery groups. The form of its arrival and flowering is as varied as are the people of the earth. God's salvific Being moves in very personal ways. The personal, infinitely varied, divine energy of salvation touches us each in response to our specific needs. Like the force of a magnet that imbues all of creation, it draws all of us, through our particular circumstances, symbols, practices, and thought-structures, into the heart of God. In very personal ways, all are loved into becoming the fullness of what we are created to be. In the end, all are made free by the One who creates all.

5

Setting Jesus Free

The gate is narrow and the road is hard that leads
to life, and there are few who find it.
—Jesus (Matt. 7:14)

Jesus stands at the center of Christianity. In one way or another, every time we gather for worship as a church, we proclaim our faith in him. When our religion functions like a closed cult, faith in Jesus accomplishes one thing: it helps us maintain an imaginary parallel religious world that is closed in on itself. In this parallel world Jesus is kept in a prison of sorts. He is brought out, gagged and bound, and only allowed to speak in limited ways that confirm his role as a litmus test for the group that is "saved." Alternatively, Jesus may be kept in the prison of domestication. Here he is confined to the role of a comforting friend whose sole purpose is to keep our pietistic feelings intact.

But when we allow Jesus to point out toward the specifics of our experience and the universal nature of human life, our faith in him accomplishes something quite different. When we look to Jesus' teachings and their costly applications to our real life struggles, Jesus comes alive. When we take on the stories and life patterns of Jesus as our own story and life pattern, he is set free.

WHAT IS IT ABOUT HIM?

Most of the people that I know have an affection for Jesus. Buddhists, Jews, ex-Roman Catholics, skeptical agnostics, and atheists often have a warm spot in their hearts for this carpenter rabbi. They may not believe in the teachings about him, they may not like the church, but they like Jesus. Part of this is our human need for a hero. We all want someone we can look up to. Historically, Jesus has been the primary hero for the majority of people in the Western world. But part of the affection for this man is also his particular character. Beneath the church and its teachings, beneath the ravings of televangelists, beneath the hurt that people have suffered in Jesus' name, often lies a residual love for the human character of Jesus himself.

When I ask what it is about Jesus' character that is so persistently compelling, several qualities emerge. He not only spoke about love, he loved fully—especially the people whom others wouldn't love. He was tough; he stood up to injustice and hypocrisy. His wisdom about life and its priorities was profoundly simple and clear. He was sure of God's goodness and nearness. He healed. He always cut through to the heart of the matter. He was streetwise about people and yet retained his humility and gentleness. He was a brilliant teacher, using simple yet powerful parables. Whether this in fact describes the way Jesus actually was all of the time is another matter. For those who feel affection for Jesus, it is enough that he seemed to possess many of the characteristics which they feel enlightened, compassionate, and wise heroes ought to possess.

The problem for those outside the church, as well as for many inside the church, is all the other stuff surrounding him. Certain sayings and actions attributed to Jesus in the Gospels don't fit the characteristics admired. Some of the teachings about him in the Epistles seem to conflict with the image that is carried by the admirer. Various doctrines of the church regarding Jesus appear to be irrelevant if not bizarre.

In the Gospels, Jesus insists upon adherence to the Law. He forbids divorce. He warns cities of their ultimate destruction because of their rejection of him. A Samaritan woman's plea for the healing of her daughter is initially spurned by Jesus with an insult. Jesus requires others to believe in him. He seems obsessed with his coming betrayal and death. In the Epistles, salvation through belief in Christ seems to become more important than either his teachings or his character. Jesus' death on the cross is interpreted as a necessary bloody sacrifice. In his name, sexual immorality and a host of other sins are condemned. Little of this fits the image of the enlightened hero to which the admirer holds.

And then we get into the doctrines of the church. Christ existed as the second person of the Godhead, prior to his human life. His birth was a coming to earth of the eternal God, planned and executed in a desire to save a fallen race from destruction.

When he died, a cosmic ransom took place. After his death, his body ascended into heaven. There, he sits at God the Father's right hand in glory. He will come back at the end of time to judge all.

What does any of this have to do with Jesus' simple, clear teachings about humility and the need to forgive one's enemy?

In writing the New Testament, its authors never sat down to record accurately what Jesus said and did. They freely mixed and altered several elements: oral traditions about Jesus which had developed over a generation or more, retrojected interpretations of earlier and older scriptures, and their own new sayings and events that were designed to teach and correct an emerging church as it struggled through ecclesiastical and doctrinal controversies. The Gospels were an art form from the word go, not a set of history books unfortunately tampered with by later meddlers. The picture and even the specific words of Jesus are hopelessly mingled with the subjective point of view of the authors. There is not available to us, and never has been, a pure rendering of Jesus that is separable from the rest.

For some, this knowledge is the beginning of cynicism. What is the point of believing in something that is merely an opinionated faith statement? It must be remembered that behind this created picture of Jesus lay a real experience. It may be impossible to recover specific knowledge of what was actually said and done, but we know that the experience was there. Jesus really lived. In his life he had an experience of God that was real. Those who followed Jesus had a transformative experience of God through him. They came up against Jesus' character, his being, and came to know God in a new way. In turn, those who wrote the theology of the emerging church had an experience of a new kind of encounter with God through Jesus. Furthermore, those who follow Jesus now also have a real and life changing experience. All of this is very real.

So the Gospels emerged from experience. They, and the church's theology about Jesus (Christology) attempt to lead us, too, back into real experience. As such, the Gospels and Christology are forms that mediate an encounter with God. They can mediate something very real that Jesus, his disciples, the early church, and the saints through the centuries have all been affected by.

We must not be naïve, attempting to seize upon the sayings of the "real" Jesus uncovered by biased biblical scholarship. Nor must we be so ingenuous as to embrace wholeheartedly the teaching of the church as a description of objective and historical reality. Neither does it help to be cynical. We can miss the Christian experience of eternal life which millions have been affected by if we dismiss the form as an inaccurate, biased report of something that is lost to history. If we are to follow Jesus, we must be wise as serpents, innocent as doves. It helps to understand the historical development of our inherited picture of him.

EARLY VIEWS

Shortly after his death, Jesus' followers began to ask themselves "Who was he, and what was he about?" He was not like any teacher, any person for that matter, that they had ever known. They began to ponder his identity. There was something mysteriously otherworldly about him, which was behind the fresh experience that had affected them. Their Christology was an attempt to answer their own questions about their experience with Jesus.

By looking at the development of their questions and answers, we can see a progressively higher and higher view of Jesus. We can trace, through the New Testament and the creeds of the early fourth century, a gradual shift in the church's subjective view of Jesus. The use of Christology became an extension of the art form of the Gospels. It was a way of continuing to paint the picture of their very real faith experience. The picture evolved over time.

Paul, who wrote the earliest and also least biographical words about Jesus, had never met him, except in a vision. Paul's letters contain no parables, no descriptions of Jesus' birth, resurrection, or other events. Paul's concern is pastoral rather than doctrinal. He simply wrote letters to the small, struggling churches he helped found. He wants to help followers of Jesus progress in their faith journey. But through his pastoral letters, he expressed his Christology.

Most of the time for Paul, Jesus seemed to be subordinate to God. As Christ is the head of the church, God is the head of Jesus. Paul did refer to Jesus as the Lord, but we must be careful with our use of this and other terms. We live on the other side of the creeds from Paul. We hear the term "Lord" and we think "God." But the use of the term "Lord" in the New Testament was not so absolute. Lord was, at times, something akin to "master," "sir," or "teacher." For Paul to say that there was one Lord, Jesus Christ, may have been to say that for Christians, Jesus is our only real master and teacher.

Paul's highest Christology comes in his understanding of the resurrection. In this event Jesus was shown to be something more than the rest of us mortals. God glorified him in his resurrection. But the main point of Paul's emphasis upon this was not so much to lead us to worship a glorified Jesus as to put our faith in him by joining him in his death, resurrection, and glorification. Since Paul's main concern for the churches to whom he wrote was pastoral, he emphasized the effect of living in Christ. To believe in Jesus was a way of participating in what Jesus experienced. Just as Jesus, our guide and master, found unity with God through his death and resurrection, we find unity with God through a spiritual death and resurrection of faith. Paul's was a pastoral Christology of mystical participation in the reality that Christ lived out.

The Gospel of Mark was the earliest of the four. In this Gospel, Jesus' humanity is emphasized. He is tempted, he asserts that "only God is good" (Mark 10:18), he is forsaken, and he is not omniscient. He is, however, filled with the spirit of God, and so he is able to do superhuman acts. In his baptism he seems to be adopted as God's Son. Going back behind the high Christology of the creeds once again, we must ask what that term meant. Was it meant to convey the second person of the Trinity or the Son in the sense of God's emissary or representative?

Matthew and Luke were written later. Their chief addition to Mark's Christology is the birth narratives. Now there is a miraculous virgin birth, a sign of his differentness even before his baptism. He is God's Son right from the start. This is driven home in the story of Jesus, at the age of twelve, astounding the elders in the temple, and explaining to his distraught parents that they needn't have worried about his absence. He was merely in his father's house.

In John, the latest of the Gospels, we see a quantum leap forward in Christology. Jesus is eternal, existing both before his human birth and at the end of time. He is the source of life, spiritual nurture, salvation, and light. He is one with God. If we have seen Jesus, we have seen God. Having postcreedal ears, we hear this to mean that Jesus is God. But that's not what is said. John has Jesus proclaiming his unity with God and saying that God is completely visible through him. There is a difference between this and the much later, even higher Christological statement of the Nicene Creed, which asserts that Jesus is "true God from true God . . . of one Being with the Father."

Some passages, some books of the New Testament are more concerned with Jesus' faithfulness, his teachings, and his humanity and love. Others emphasize the effects of living in Jesus. Still other New Testament authors speak of his identity in God, focusing on his nature. In the earliest Gospel, Jesus demands faith in God alone. In the last Gospel there is a demand for faith in Jesus himself. The early church, during the half-century that the New Testament was being written, gradually moved to a higher Christology.

Jesus Becomes God

Various Christologies developed over the next four hundred years, most of them concerned with the relationship between Christ's two natures. Some emphasized his humanity, some his divinity. These may seem to be silly philosophical arguments that have no relevance for us. But at the heart of the Christological controversy was a basic difference of opinion about how God is involved in life. This argument goes way back. It is an ancient, universal dichotomy between transcendence and immanence. We see this difference reflected right away in the Bible, in the first chapters of Genesis; there are two creation stories. We see this same argument represented in the two views of Plato and Aristotle. Later, immersed in the Mediterranean philosophical milieu, early theologians of the church continued, in a Christological form, this old discussion. This argument is still with us today, and affects all religious seekers more than we realize.

One side says that God is profoundly immanent; God comes into our awareness through the very stuff of this life. Like the God of the second creation narrative in Genesis, God is with us. God walks in the garden with Adam and Eve, and they know his presence in their midst. Prior to Christianity, Aristotle came from a similar point of view. For him, reality was to be observed and known in what is before us in the natural world. What you see is what you get. In terms of Christology, this means that God was revealed in the humanity of Jesus. Jesus was filled with God from within his human nature. We see God in the life of a man. This became known as Christology from below, or a low Christology. This is the Christology to which, perhaps obviously, I hold.

The other side in the Christological debate emphasized transcendence. God, who is essentially apart from this life, directs and occasionally enters this life from above. Like the God of the first account of creation in Genesis, God is powerful enough to simply speak in order for things to come into being. In pre-Christian philosophy, Plato corresponds to this point of view. For Plato, reality exists in perfect essence somewhere apart from nature. Nature's forms can only represent and point to these essences. Translated into Christology, this means that God came down from heaven and inhabited a human form. Jesus was, in a sense, a divine visitor who entered this realm for a short time, and then returned to his real home. This is called Christology from above, or a high Christology.

It is our loss that, in the socio-political events of the early Middle Ages that overtook the church, Christological debate virtually ended in 451. Shortly afterwards, the stable structure of the Roman Empire lay in ruins, and the church was less able to continue to hold its public, state-sponsored councils. Gone, in this social chaos, was the state church and its open councils of debate. The result of this was that the Nicene Creed of 325 and the Chalcedonian statement of 451 became the last word on Christ for centuries. The creeds became fixed definitions of Christ. We have inherited these frozen statements. The church often acts as if those four hundred years of debate, immersed in a Greek philosophical, prescientific and prepsychological atmosphere, was sufficient for all time. It is a common assumption that the creeds settled the question of Christ. Many treat the creeds as if they were more important than scripture, more important than prayer and the experience of the living God. This is creedal fundamentalism.

The history books tell us that in the creedal councils, culminating in Chalcedon in 451, the church ended up making a wise political and philosophical move. They ostensibly said yes to both sides of the debate. Christ is both fully human and divine. In Christ dwelt both the transcendence of God and the immanence of mankind. An unresolvable paradox was held forth, like a koan for meditation through the ages. The mystery of God was left as a mystery. But what really happened is that Christology from above won out. Having made a slow but inevitable march toward a higher and higher view of Christ, the church finally moved Jesus' divinity from a man who is filled with God into the Creator coming down to earth.

Remember where we started. Nowhere in the New Testament does Jesus say that he is God. Specifically, he rebukes one who calls him good, saying that only God is good. He prays to God, who is both our Father and his Father. Jesus is adopted as God's faithful son, as his emissary. He is a man who is subordinate to but also one with God, filled with God's spirit. In his life, death, and resurrection Jesus' followers saw God fully revealed. We begin with the scriptures here. We end up with Jesus dwelling in heaven before his birth and coming down to take on a human form. High Christology won. If you doubt this, just look at what is suspect as heresy even now. To say that Jesus was a man who was one with and transparent to God is to invite raised eyebrows in some quarters of the church. But to say that Jesus is God and to pray to him as such is commonplace. This would never be called heresy.

And so the church evolved in its view of Jesus during those formative centuries. We are left with the legacy. Why did this evolution take place, and why is this legacy perpetuated even today? Mainstream theologians tell us that the Holy Spirit, over those four hundred years, lead the church into a fuller understanding of Christ's nature, even fuller than Jesus' own understanding during his lifetime! I think that there is a more basic, human reason for the victory of high Christology: we put Jesus on a pedestal in order to keep him safely at a distance. It is easier to worship Jesus than to follow him.

Jesus knew his own unity with God, without a doubt. He was beyond dualism. Jesus said that this unity, and the extraordinary things he did, were possible for those with faith. He prayed that we would be one with God even as he was. He asked that we know the fullness of joy and glory in God that he knew. But it is easier for us to see ourselves as forever separate and sinful.

To see our unity with God would mean that we would learn to move through our sins, our relative separateness, with the confidence of those who know who they really are. It is easier to worry, to be weak, and to lean on the rescuing power of God. To see our unity with God necessitates that we practice a form of prayer that gives us an experience of that unity. It is easier to ask God for help, to have a conversation. To see our oneness means that we revere God's presence in all our feelings, actions, bodily sensations, and thoughts. It is easier to make Jesus into the only place we need to look for God.

Jesus called us to see the immediacy, the incarnation of God in this life. He pointed to God's kingdom everywhere. Jesus called his followers to see the beauty and challenge of this incarnation in their everyday lives. But it is easier for us not to rise to this challenge. It is easier to make Jesus the alpha and omega of God's kingdom. It is easier to make Jesus the only Incarnation of God.

Jesus also called us to die with him. Referring to his own inevitable arrest and crucifixion (which he knew would only be a matter of time), Jesus said that we have to take up our cross daily and follow him if we are to be his disciples. It is easier to make Jesus' death on the cross a pietistic wonder. Lost in our sins, rescued by the precious blood of his sacrifice, we are grateful. We may be grateful, but are we willing to pick up our own cross daily? To do so means that we must learn how to die daily to our fears and self-centered ambitions, our aversions and attractions. To take up our cross daily means that we enter the emptiness of our heart and die there, like Jesus did. It is easier to glorify the cross of Christ. It is easier to believe in the cross than to take it up.

I am not saying that all those who interchange Christ with God are idolatrous. It is possible, and quite common, to worship Jesus, and to *also* faithfully follow him where he leads. The church is replete with those who do just that. It is a question of whether our worship of Jesus gets in the way of seeing our divinity in his humanity, or following him. The church all too often provides an easy out: a dualism that keeps Jesus and his challenges at a safe distance. The church has erred by overemphasizing high Christology. In doing so, she provides an opportunity to pietize the vibrancy and strength of the gospel of Jesus. Through her theology about Jesus, she has domesticated him.

I believe that Jesus was divine. But Jesus' divinity was that of a man completely filled with and transparent to God. His clear wisdom, his miracles, his resurrection, and his effect upon me and others are proof enough for me of God's full presence in him. In this way Jesus is different from me and from any man or woman I have ever known. He was one with God in a very unique way. But Jesus also promised and challenged us to the same fullness and transparency. By following the path he showed us, we participate in his death, resurrection, and also his divinity.

It is for this reason that I am much more comfortable with the traditional liturgical formula which prays "through Jesus Christ our Lord," rather than praying to him. We, like Jesus, pray to God. But Christians pray through the reality that Jesus has brought us into. We pray through this kingdom, this unity, and incarnation which he has made known to us. We pray through Jesus because he has mediated our experience of God.

In the end, it may not make much difference whether we say that Jesus is God or that Jesus' divinity comes from his humanity being filled with God's Spirit. In a sense the two points of view, high and low Christology, meet in the place where we simply hold Christ as the one who for us fully revealed God's nature as well as our redeemed human nature. What is really important, however, as Jesus taught, is not what we believe in our thoughts but how we live our life. Jesus was more concerned in the end with his followers actually following him on his path.

THE WAY

*F*inding the Jesus path requires that we look at the big picture of scripture and theology, and not get stuck on the details. We must listen for the patterns, even the ones we don't understand or feel comfortable with. We must take the letter of the Law with a grain of salt and the spirit of the Law with deadly seriousness. We can't listen too much with our head, lest we get sidetracked on secondary and passing concerns. We have to listen with our heart in order to go to the heart of the matter.

I am reminded of the difficult time of my life during seminary, when I often felt quite alienated from the church into which I was soon to be ordained. I frequently sought out the advice and counsel of the few clergy whom I saw as role models, those who followed the Jesus path with integrity and breadth. One of these clergy said that I would need to use night vision. To put it mildly, this puzzled me at the time, but it has become a real anchor for me since then. Faith requires that we look patiently and quietly through the shapes and forms of the night in order to see what is, in fact, directly in front of us. We need to listen and watch with our heart, not necessarily trusting the distractions of our fears and thoughts.

When we use this kind of vision to look at the big patterns of scripture and theology, we can see, beneath the subjective limitations and agendas, beneath the impulse to keep Jesus at a divine distance, the light of the gospel. It still shines through. It is as if the authors of scripture and theology had an experience of unfiltered light in Jesus. As they tried to put this into words, they applied layers of cultural and psychological form to give it shape, so that others could see it. The light became filtered as it passed through the layers. But the light is still visible, through the layers of the form. In fact, it is only visible to most of us because others before us put it into a form which we could see and use. Without form, as limited as it can be, we cannot see the light.

Theological and biblical form is highly symbolic, mystical, and always subjective. Inevitably it can only suggest the mystery that lies beyond. But the light which is visible through it is an objective reality. It has a particular quality about it that is consistent for all those who experience it. If we come to know the gospel light in our lives as the authors of scripture and the creeds knew it in theirs, it will be the same light. As

God responded when Moses asked what he should call this God, "I am who I am."

Jesus spoke about, more than anything else, the kingdom of God, the kingdom of heaven. It is a constant image, woven throughout the Gospels. This kingdom is near us, within us, and among us. It is the reality and quality of God's presence in this life. The kingdom is God's immediacy, judgment, and love. Jesus uses a great variety of natural, ordinary images to drive home this his most basic teaching. The kingdom of God is fertile, contrasted with rocky soil; the wheat amongst the weeds; a mustard seed that grows into a great tree; a treasure buried in a field; a wide net that is cast into the sea, separating good from evil. The kingdom is the open quality of children; the unconditional forgiveness of the prodigal son's father; the freedom from attachment to which Jesus called the rich young man; the extravagance of paying every worker the same, no matter how long they have worked. The kingdom is a wedding banquet to which all are invited but few respond; the unexpected arrival of a master, who finds some servants asleep and some awake; the separation of sheep from goats.

In all of these images and more, Jesus is teaching, first and foremost, that God is here and now. God is an experience of abundant life which is available to all. God is also the immediacy of judgment, of discernment and truth, that is there for all those who have ears to hear it. God is the experience of love and forgiveness. Above all, this experience is now, and is not dependent upon correct belief or behavior. It is available to all who hear and see it, at every moment. This part of the Jesus path is what we follow when we are awake in life. Seeing the kingdom of heaven is coming face to face with the heart stopping truth that life is full of God. It is knowing that we live in a sacred world.

One afternoon some years ago my family and I went for a drive to Bosque del Apache, a wildlife sanctuary south of Albuquerque. The Bosque is a large wetland area along the Rio

Grande, a stopping off place for millions of birds every year on their migration route. Toward the end of our visit, we rounded a corner and encountered an incredible sight. The sun was going down over the nearby mountains, and it was spreading its soft orange light through puffy cumulus clouds. Shadows were long and the light was so clear that everything seemed very close, as if you could touch objects a great ways off. Everything stood out as distinct, super-real, and electric. On the meadow in front of us stood thousands of white Canada snow geese, all facing the sunset, as if in prayer, giving praise to the God of light. We stood still and silent. All four of us were transfixed. It was as if we had suddenly been transported to heaven. All of us—the clouds, the sun, the mountains, the snow geese, we four humans—were lifted up for a moment and held together, and we all knew it. The sun dipped below the mountain and as if on command, the snow geese suddenly flew up into the air with a loud cry in one graceful and swift movement, forming a shrieking, swirling cloud directly overhead. I cried, my son wet his pants, and we all were knocked senseless. We all knew something had happened.

Who can explain such moments? They just happen. We see the abundant glory of God in this world. This is, I am convinced, how life is all of the time. We just don't usually have the eyes to see it. But when we are graced with these moments, we see the kingdom of God, which is all around us and within us, always and everywhere. Jesus lived in this place and preached about it to all who would hear it. Contemplative prayer seeks to awaken us to this reality.

The church has held out the kingdom of heaven in the concrete immediacy of this life through its teaching of the incarnation. Primarily this doctrine has to do with the presence of God in Jesus' life, in the midst of this everyday world. But this teaching also goes deeper. The incarnation, in the broadest sense, is about the sacredness of the world: the presence of God in all that has been created. The Christian church in the sacramental tradition is extremely worldly; we always worship God through the use of material objects and sensations. We see the sacred in bread and wine, oil, fire, and water. We utilize the ordinary senses: hearing music; smelling incense; touching each other in the laying on of hands and the kiss of peace; eating bread and drinking wine; seeing the colors of vestments, flowers, and stained glass. All the sacraments are sensory experiences. This is because the incarnation of God is so primary for the church. God is in this ordinary world of the senses. It is through this world that we see the glory of God's kingdom.

Jesus' preaching about the kingdom of heaven and the incarnation of God in ordinary life was a threat to the religious authorities, who always like to think that the institution in which they hold power possesses the keys to such experiences. Jesus pointed to its free availability to all. But what got him into even more trouble was his preaching about his unity with God. This is another part of the Jesus path, which often gets identified exclusively with Jesus, but belongs to all of us. We are one with God. Jesus knew without a doubt his unity with God. We are not so sure.

Unity with God is at the heart of the miraculous birth narratives. In these, Mary experiences a mystical sexual union with God. The Holy Spirit comes upon her and the power of God overshadows her. She is impregnated by God. The prophet Isaiah is then brought to mind who referred to the birth of a child whose name was Emmanuel, which means "God is with us." Jesus' birth emanates the light of God in the form of a star in the heavens.

At Jesus' baptism, his unity with God is expressed through the voice from heaven that proclaims him as God's son, and the spirit of God, like a dove, which alights on him. In his transfiguration, his three closest disciples have a vision of him shining with light. Throughout his life he exhibits the power and the assurance of one who knows his identity in

God. He speaks as one who possesses and doesn't need to prove his authority. Jesus calls people to himself, to rest in him, so that they may experience resting in God. In the Gospel of John we see the clearest display of his known union with God. Jesus is the light, he is living water, he is bread which gives eternal life. He prays to God that his followers may know the unity with God which he knows. Finally, Jesus appears after his death, fully revealing God in his resurrected being.

Jesus never shows his unity with God in order to draw attention to himself. He does it in order to draw attention to God, who has filled him. Furthermore, he does it in order to call his followers to the same unity which he knows. Jesus promised this to his disciples. He apparently also gave them a taste of it through their exposure to him. Otherwise, why would they drop everything to follow him as they did? If Jesus' glory were for himself alone, I doubt that the disciples would have given up as much as they did, just to be in the presence of his glory. They must have also begun to realize for themselves what he promised they would know: their own unity with God.

The church celebrates this unity which we have with God primarily through the sacrament of baptism and through the accompanying rite of the renewal of baptismal vows. In baptism and baptismal renewal we remember who we are: sons and daughters of God. God lives in us, and we live in God. No matter what we may do or become in our lives, this is who we are and nothing can take it away. The church also celebrates this unity through the Eucharist. In this sacrament we eat and drink the body and blood of Christ, taking into our very bloodstream the reality of God. We are literally, physically one.

Another aspect of the Jesus path is love. Knowing both the goodness of God's immanence in this ordinary world and his unity with God, Jesus was able to love unconditionally. He accepted, loved and spent time with those whom others loved to hate: Jewish tax collectors (who, in profiting from Rome's oppression of Israel, were enemies of all Jews), prostitutes, Samaritans, Pharisees, lepers, and Roman soldiers. He was seldom in respectable company. The ones he accepted were often healed by his love. While they expected and braced themselves for rejection, Jesus surprised them by coming to them on their terms and loving them where they were. Jesus taught about love through dozens of parables. He modeled and taught about forgiveness, the unconditional acceptance of who we are, right now. This forgiveness is lavish, free, and unearned. It just is.

To say that God loves us and forgives us is not necessarily to regress back into anthropomorphism, making God into a person like you and me. God is love. God is the power and force of this reality in the universe. Everything works when love is given room to be. This is just the way things are made. We are made to love. When we hate, we cause chaos and we hurt ourselves, others, and creation. We know God's love and forgiveness to the extent that we live in the reality of what is. We can ask for it, invite it, and accept it, because God's energy of love and acceptance for who we are emanates ceaselessly out of Being.

The love which Jesus displayed and to which he calls his followers is a radical openness to the other. We must be wise as serpents and not let ourselves or others be abused, but we are called to eventually drop beneath our fears and preconceptions and see the other where they are. We are called to hear their pain, to understand them. We are especially called to go to those who are marginalized in our society, who are told over and over of their inferiority and unacceptability. Jesus calls us to go into the prisons, the homes of our gay and lesbian neighbors, the AIDS wards, the homeless shelters, the nursing homes, and the drug treatment centers. Without condescension, without preaching at them, we are to be with them on their terms, as Jesus was.

It is easy to romanticize those who do this well. We put people like Mother Teresa on a pedestal and marvel at her saintliness.

I couldn't do that, we say. There was a wonderful documentary film about Mother Teresa, in which the reporters and others who followed her around gave her this kind of distancing adulation. Mother Teresa is nobody's fool, and when this would happen she'd turn directly to her admirer, and with a twinkle in her eye, gently remind them that they no doubt had plenty of opportunity, right where they lived, to practice the same kind of compassion. Surely, she said, there must be someone in your family, your neighborhood, or your workplace who needs your love. Just love them. Her admirer would often slink off, chagrined.

Jesus also calls us to forgive ourselves and to forgive those who have hurt us. This is not an easy thing. Sometimes it takes years of working through hatred to get to forgiveness. But we take the stance that faces us toward this goal. We don't necessarily feel loving, but we drop our demonizing and we love through understanding. This love and forgiveness is the power of God running through us, and it heals. When we love and forgive, we are participating in God's life, and we are one; for God is this energy of love. When we learn to forgive ourselves, we move out of the captivity of shame and fear.

The church practices this love and forgiveness in a wide variety of ways. Sometimes she is more faithful to this call than others. But the church does have a long history of hospital care, work with the dying, prison ministry, peace and justice efforts, feeding the hungry, and assisting the poor. We wash one another's feet every Maundy Thursday, as Jesus did that same night, to remind ourselves of our servanthood. The church also holds out the sacrament of reconciliation, or confession. In this rite we take, in a formal setting, the stance of forgiveness toward ourselves and others.

It is the context of God's unconditional love and ready forgiveness that makes possible another part of the Jesus path—judgment. Unfortunately, the church has often taught judgmentalism and condemnation, which is part of the reason why we blanch at the sound of this word: judgment. But we also blanch because we don't always like the truth about ourselves. Judgment is standing naked before God and seeing ourselves as we truly are. This can be uncomfortable. But it is something we can endure and even embrace when done in the context of unconditional love. The model of a good parent is helpful here. When I call my sons on the carpet and tell them what I see in their behavior, I am judging them. I am using discernment to judge with the truth. I say what I have to say (when I occasionally do it well) with clarity, without emotionally communicating my disapproval of their being. They are not crushed because I do not condemn them as people. They know I love them. Similarly, God's judgment is given while we are being held in the arms of love.

Jesus judged. His words were not always comfortable. He pointed out to the religious leaders their hypocrisy. He reminded a certain crowd of their own sin, men who were poised to stone to death an adulterous woman. He said that his followers were more like family to him than his own mother and siblings, who thought he was crazy. He told us that we too might have to separate ourselves from those we love if they stand between us and God. Outraged, Jesus caused a near riot in the temple when he lashed out at the moneychangers who took economic advantage of religious pilgrims who had to pay for their sacrifice in the local currency. He reminded the woman at the well of her inability to stay in a relationship. Jesus thereby made a link between her lack of commitment in love and her expressed need for spiritual, living water. Jesus showed the rich young man who wanted eternal life that he was attached to his wealth, and this was getting in the way. He told us we'd all be judged by God, that the chaff and the wheat, the sheep and the goats, would be separated.

I had an experience of judgment some twenty years ago which I will never forget. It only took a moment, but I was laid bare in the context of love. I was visiting an old girlfriend at her house near Monterey. I had come over just for the evening, in order to attend a party at her house. That night, there would be a long, windy drive home through the foggy Santa Cruz mountains. I was nervous about being at her house, and probably angry with myself for even going there. Consequently, I stood at the drink table and poured myself a large glass of champagne, downed it, and poured another. A young man stood across the table. He was a large, bearded, plaid-shirted, kindly bear of a man. In a look that shot right through me, he quietly but firmly said "Take it easy." I froze inside. I had been seen. I had been found out. I had been judged. But it was done in love, because he knew that I'd need my wits for the drive home. He didn't want me to hurt myself or others, and so he applied loving judgment. It may have saved my life.

The church provides judgment when it lives out its prophetic witness to individuals and the world. There are times when parishioners must be told that they are hating, that they are hurting themselves and others. The church can and occasionally does bar from communion those who are living lives of notorious evil, who have badly hurt others, or who are living in hatred. This is called excommunication. Socially, the church exercises its ministry of judgment when it speaks and acts prophetically about social and political circumstances. When injustice is seen, Christians have a responsibility to protest and stand in its way. Part of walking on the path of Jesus is using our God-given judging function.

Finally, when we tread the path of Jesus , we practice the way of death and resurrection. The accounts of Jesus' death and resurrection take up a large portion of each of the Gospels, and this is for a good reason. They lie at the heart of what Jesus is about. Throughout his ministry, Jesus reminded his followers of the fact that he was going to die and rise again. He would be betrayed by someone close to him, arrested and crucified, and the whole thing would seemingly go down in flames. Since the resurrection was a mystery beyond their comprehension, this talk about death was hard to hear. All their hopes for the success of their shared mission were jeopardized by this talk, and so they chose not to hear it. As often as Jesus brought it up, they didn't understand it and they pushed it out of their consciousness.

Jesus also taught the necessity of dying and rising in other ways. A seed could not become a plant unless it died off the vine and fell to the ground. A woman must go through the anguish and pain of labor prior to the joy of bringing a human being into the world. Jesus told his followers that they would have to take up their cross daily in order to be his disciples. A child dies and Jesus brings her back to life. Lazarus too.

In all this talk about death and resurrection, Jesus held out the essential truth about spiritual regeneration. We must suffer and die in order to be reborn. There is no way around it. The Israelites went through spiritual death in the Red Sea and in their years of wandering in the desert before entering the Promised Land. The psalmist spoke of going through, not around, the valley of the shadow of death prior to dwelling in the house of the Lord. The desert fathers and mothers went off into the emptiness of the Egyptian desert in order to die and be reborn. The alcoholic hits bottom before turning toward life and hope. In contemplative prayer, our separating patterns of control and manipulation die in order that we might experience the freedom that lies beyond them. The hell of childhood abuse must be faced before the goodness of a mature life can be known.

Spiritual and emotional growth is dependent upon dying to self. The ego, which always wants to control and have things its way, must die. All our attachments, preferences, carefully protected fears, and our ideas about how our life should be must be crucified on the cross of life as it comes to us. The alternative is to go on protecting the ego's little world, which is a hellish illusion. When we manage to allow this dying to take place, a life rises up in us that is not our own doing. It is the nature of life itself, the goodness and fresh quality of life as it is in God. This is resurrection.

Ultimately, this is why the Jesus path is not a matter of imitation. We cannot accomplish what we are called to be and do as followers of Jesus: to live in God's here-and-now kingdom of immediacy, to be one with God, to love and to forgive, and to stand unashamedly under God's healing judgment. We cannot do it because the ego, with which we try to be holy, is the very problem. The more we try to live the Jesus path, the more we come up against our inability to do it. The ego and its effort must die as we realize our limits and learn to surrender to God. This point of surrender is where the grace of God begins. For it is only possible for God to work when our working stops, and it is only possible to be found when we realize that we are lost. Resurrection does not come through our holy efforts to be an imitator of Jesus; it comes through crucifixion. We must come, again and again, to the point of not knowing, of hitting bottom, of utter emptiness before God. Here is the place of salvation, for here is where God's hidden and uncontrollable power begins to move. The fact that we cannot succeed in the spiritual path of Jesus without dying and being raised is what is meant by salvation by faith rather than works.

The church observes this central reality of the faith in the most important time of the church year: Holy Week and Easter. In this annual drama, we re-enact Jesus' journey through death to rebirth. We join him on this path. This is done every year so that we can remember just how important it is. Over time it sinks into our thick skulls that this re-enactment is not just about Jesus. It is about us. Then we can begin to look at our dying with interest instead of repulsion, with acceptance and even welcome. This too is an illogical part of the Jesus path. It just doesn't make sense, in our success driven culture, to willingly surrender to suffering and death of the self as Jesus did. But if we don't, suffering and the ego will always control us. We will always fear pain, and the inevitable disappointments, failures, and tragedies of life will doggedly mar our happiness; we will always fear loss of control, and this will, paradoxically, control us.

In the Gospels, we have a constellation of qualities, sayings, and events which together comprise a historical and artistic rendering of an experience. We call this experience Jesus Christ. When we say "Jesus Christ, the Only Son of God" we are naming not only a person but a universal experience which the Gospels attempt to capture on paper. All those who come to know this reality in their lives, by whatever name, live in what we call Christ. This experience has an identifiable, objective quality which is not simply whatever we want it to be. Jesus, and his universal path, both have a particular character.

My (or anyone else's) description of this character is certainly colored by subjective opinion. But through life experience, study, exposure to others who have walked this path, and reflection upon how this path is found in other forms, we come to see its shape. Its shape, as far as I can see it, is this: awakening to the fresh immediacy of God-in-life now; accepting our ultimate unity with God; giving and receiving love and forgiveness; standing under the judgment of God's truth and using our judging function to discern injustice in the world; and embracing suffering and spiritual death as the path to resurrection.

Practicing Christians are not the only ones who walk the Jesus path. Many others show their faith in this path by their dedication to his way of life. All who live this way are, in fact, followers of the Jesus path. They believe in Jesus, by virtue of the way they faith. Jesus himself said, "The tree is known by its fruit" (Matt. 12:33) and "I know my own and my own know me. . . . I have other sheep, that do not belong to this fold" (John 10:14, 16).

To recognize Jesus' path in the myriad forms that it takes in this life is to set Jesus free from the shackles of the church. We have for too long treated him as a possession, as if belief in certain ideas about him enabled us to live in a right relationship with him, and to thereby make him our own. Jesus asked no such thing of his followers. He didn't care much about what they thought of him. But he cared passionately how they were in relationship to God, to one another, and how they lived. When we recognize the universal yet specific path of Jesus as belonging to the wideness of God's creation, finding many forms, we free him from the limits of Christian piety and culture. We let him be where he was during his walk on earth: in life.

Why, then, profess oneself as a Christian? Why go to church? Because for those who recognize the Jesus path as the way of life, the Christian church is a powerful source of contact with this way. Through the sacraments, biblical study, ministry in the name (the way) of Christ, fellowship with other followers, and prayerful meditation on the symbols and stories of this path, we are encouraged and strengthened for the journey.

To Faith in Jesus

*F*aith in Jesus is central to Christianity. But what do we mean by this? Do we mean that we believe certain assertions about him? Surely it is more than this. When we limit our faith to theological positions we are living in our heads. When our faith is only about metaphysical realities, it doesn't make much of a connection with the way we experience our everyday life.

By faith in Jesus do we mean that he is a "great guy," someone everyone should look up to, right alongside all the other great religious teachers? Surely it is more than this. To simply respect him as one "great guy" among many others is to dwell in the no-mans-land of religious multiplicity. To belong everywhere is to belong nowhere. The world of mythologies is extremely interesting and can bring depth and breadth to one's chosen path, but it's not a practice that can change one's life. To live in the ocean of comparative religion can be an intellectual, pallid thing.

The word for "faith" in New Testament Greek is a verb. It is not something we have; it is something we do. To "faith in Jesus" means that we walk the path that he walked. When we say that we are Christian, we also say that we are "followers" of Christ. If we don't follow him along his path, how can we be a follower? Jesus promised his followers the experience of the immediacy of God in their lives, the kingdom of heaven. He said that those who followed him would know this kingdom, that it is not limited to an afterlife: it breaks into this one. Jesus also promised his followers the rocklike stability and peace that comes from knowing that we are one with God, as he did. He said we would know the love and forgiveness of God. But none of this is possible without walking the path that he walked.

In a sobering passage of the Gospel of Matthew (25:31–46), Jesus describes the fate of those who actually follow him and those who don't. He gets quite concrete. There are those who feed the hungry, give the thirsty something to drink, welcome the stranger, clothe the naked, take care of the sick, and visit the prisoner. There are those who don't. Those who do will come to know the blessedness of God. Those who don't will come to know separation from God. He doesn't say that those who disbelieve certain theological assertions about him will be separated out. He says that to do what he did is to show faith in him, and to reap its natural consequences.

To faith in Jesus means that we surrender to and stake our life on his path. Jesus demanded everything of his disciples. If they weren't willing to drop what stood in the way of following him, they were left behind, at least for the moment. A rich young man is unwilling to part with his wealth, which stands in his way. Another wants to go and bury his father first. Someone else has to go and say goodbye to those at home. For many, what Jesus asks is too much. To all of them, Jesus responds that the kingdom of God requires total dedication. It does no good to put our hand to the plow and then look back.

We find any number of reasons why we can't surrender to this path just yet. This one person is unlovable. That one act is unforgivable. I can't embrace this particular suffering and death to self. I am unwilling to look at the truth of this one part of myself. God can't be immediately present in that area of my life. This one thing I do that I know separates me from God, I must continue.

While all of this may be true on any given day, it doesn't have to be ultimately true. We are always given another opportunity to look into our life. We are always given another opportunity to surrender on deeper and deeper levels. I often feel as though my surrender to the Jesus path is like unpeeling an onion. No matter how vulnerable I feel, sooner or later another dry, dying layer will appear, needing to be removed to expose the next layer of vulnerability.

I am convinced that the extent to which we surrender ourselves to the Jesus path will be the measure of our happiness in this life. And in the next life? Who knows. I've not been there. But it is difficult for me to imagine that life will come to a crashing halt at our death. Jesus' continuing existence after his death, witnessed by his followers, tells me that life goes on in some form. I confess that I am much more a believer in purgatory than in heaven and hell. After all, why should the next life be different in nature from this one? Our nature in this life is to gradually move forward in grace, toward our enlightenment in God. I not sure if any of us will know complete, permanent, unwavering enlightenment in this life. This means that our gradual progress will carry forward into the next. Continuing to walk on the path of life which is laid before all of creation, I imagine that we will seek, and be drawn into, an ever deeper experience of God. Our journey on the Jesus path is eternal.

6

God's Body

*Great rock statues of sitting and standing Buddhas
charged with Dharma body . . . a clarity explodes
from the rock, more than clarity of the eye . . . it is
clarity of the heart, clarity arising from a radical
expansion of self and from a renewed compassion
that brings with it a sense of belonging to all
matter, to all life, to all being. The tall stone
Buddha figures are companions ushering
one into a comonwealth without bounds.*
—Thomas Merton, describing ancient
Buddhist sites in Sri Lanka

An experiential faith will be fed by the symbols and stories
of religion's form, through awareness in prayer, and by our expanded images of God and Jesus. But for it to become fully integrated it must move into action. God must move from the
center of our being, our spiritual life, out into the world of our
body, our relationships, human community, society, and all of
the created world. God must be fully incarnated. To seek this
movement is to release the tremendous power of God from the
confines of religion into life itself.

God has a body. This body is the manifested universe
and everything that it does. All things seen and unseen are
filled with the pulsing, ever recreating life of God. There is

no dividing line between spiritual and physical, for all physical matter is nothing but energy, and energy is spirit, God's spirit of life. Just as our minds cannot be separated from our bodies, God's invisible being flows uninterrupted into impermanent physical manifestation: ever changing, evolving, being born, dying, resurrecting into mineral, plant, animal, human, relational, community, cultural, political, and historical form.

Perhaps our first awareness of God's body begins in our own bodies. But then our awareness moves outward in circles of varying radii that surround us. We get bigger and so does God as the circles move outward. Our bodies move, and we are in relation with each other all the time. And so relationships, especially in friends and family, are a vehicle for God's presence. We (and God) get bigger in community: those human groupings in which grace can be seen to move. A wider circle yet is our society: all of those in our city and beyond whose culture and brokenness affects us and whom we in turn affect. Finally, God's body is found in the widest circle of relationship: embracing all of Mother Earth, all races, all living species who share this island home.

To say that God has a body this vast is to radically extend the incarnation to its furthest limits. Christian theology proclaims that God became flesh in Jesus Christ. But the incarnation, for Christians, has never been limited to Jesus of Nazareth. As I have attempted to show, God is also enfleshed in whomever walks the same path that Jesus walked. Christian incarnational theology goes even further, however, by proclaiming that the Incarnation of Christ is symbolic of a wider and therefore greater sacramental reality; for God is seen as also incarnated in bread, wine, water, oil, touch, scripture, worship, and the love and justice that is lived out by the children of God. But this, too, is only a symbol of a greater reality; for God is incarnated in all, filling all creation with divine glory.

To say that God's body extends out from the molecular level, through family and community into society and the stars beyond is also a way of releasing God into life, where God resides. The church seems to almost assume that God can be contained in her sacraments, her scriptures, her rites, and theology. We would never say this, but by habit we act as if God is confined to the cult of the church, as if conventional congregational life says it all about God! But God is far greater, wilder, and freer than all this. Our religion is only a small expression of the Creator, for God's being is expressed in infinite form. God will not be limited by our piety or owned by whatever forms we develop, however good or useful they may be. To recognize this is to begin to see God everywhere, to release God's divine reality from its imaginary religious prison, so that God charges everything with life, direction, and love.

MATTER

*I*ronically enough, it is religion's long-time adversary, science, that has of late given us a clearer awareness of the sacredness and intelligence of creation. Scientists and theologians are talking again. Perhaps we are now moving back to a more friendly and complementary relationship between religion and science than we have enjoyed in the past few centuries in the Western world. And another, more ancient discipline — Buddhism — brings to our religious world view some striking parallels to those of physics. Through dialogue with both science and Buddhism we can see what is at the root of a contemplative Christian faith.

As Thomas Berry has said, science now gives us "a new intimacy with the universe." Fritjof Capra wrote that through physics, "The universe is no longer seen as machine, made up of a multitude of separate objects, but appears as a harmonious and indivisible whole, a network of dynamic relationships that include the human observer and his or her consciousness in an essential way." An integrated whole, all matter in the universe is interrelated. At the highest level, stars, black holes and planets move in an interdependent dance of gravity, mass, energy, and light.

Since long before modern science the Buddhists have been teaching this in what is called *dependent co-arising*. This teaching says that every action, thought, movement, breath, or event in the universe arises in the way it does because of the action of another event. This, in turn causes other events to arise. All in the universe is interdependent, and this dependency is manifested in the co-arising of actions, feelings, and events. When we dump toxic wastes, plants die. When they die, animals starve or leave. Affected by a disturbing encounter, I project my anger on to others, who are in turn affected. Calling upon the love I was given as a child, I love my children, who in turn will love others. Every thought, action, feeling, and event has both its origins and continuing manifestations in other forms. Because all is interdependent, all co-arises.

Science also turns our attention to the smallest subatomic particle. For there, physicists tell us, one can see the presence of an animating and organizing force of intelligibility which causes all to be directed toward stability and higher forms of life. Science does not prove the presence of God in creation, but it certainly seems to point to it. Organisms influence their own destinies in subjective self-organization. Similarly, in Buddhism the concept of karma says that all beings evolve within lives, from one life to the next, into higher forms of being as they work through their attachments and illusions.

Physics has also shown that all matter, because it is energy, is in a constant state of motion and change. Matter is not permanent. What may seem fixed to us is not only a swirling mass of molecules, it is also in the constant process of growth or decay. It seems that not only Jesus Christ died and rose again. The Buddhists also teach this in what is called *impermanence*; that nothing has permanence, and all is moving, changing, dying, and being reborn. Whatever thoughts, feelings, or actions we are currently in the middle of, they will pass. Much of Buddhist practice is the simple watching of these impermanent conditions as they come and go, so that we may know a freedom that is not dependent upon the passing circumstances of our life.

And so from the point of view of both modern physics and Buddhist practice, the universe is seen as a whole organism, containing within it interrelated and interdependent suborganisms; these suborganisms evolve into larger life forms, eventually producing such things as ecosystems, family, politics, and culture. There is an inherent presence of intelligence, organization, and awareness in all; all matter is energy, motion, and impermanence.

There is much here that can illuminate traditional Christian theology concerning creation. Our sense of the goodness and integrated order of God's creation, the presence of God's spirit energizing all, God's will moving creation toward wholeness, the sacredness of God's world, and the cosmic truth of the cross and resurrection are all strengthened by what contemporary physics and ancient Buddhism are teaching us.

From a Christian point of view, matter is infused, it is filled with the presence of God's. The Incarnation, which is God's body, begins with the smallest, subatomic level, in order that all creation will be made up of this basic sacred building material.

FLESH

To be a Christian who reveres God's body, we must then look to our own bodies. Inhabiting, celebrating, and caring for our own body is the beginning of our faith moving out of our heads and into the world. Before we are in a relationship, before we look to our neighbor's need, before we look to community, society, or the physical body of our planet, we must start with the first place where faith becomes incarnate for us.

We were created with a body. This is our primary experience of being in the world. A baby first lives in its bodily sensations alone: hunger, sucking milk, warmth, cold, and wet. Take a moment and look at your hand. See the protective, breathing organ that is the skin. Notice the veins that carry life giving blood even to the fingertips. Fingernails provide handy clawlike tools. Look at how the fingers articulate in three segments, and how the thumb moves in counterforce. They work together, miraculously, like a highly intelligent machine. You move it and make it do extremely complex functions without even having to think about it. Every time you pick up a pen, messages are being sent from the brain to the fingertips to guide them in the tiny, subtle, and ever-changing movements of thought we call handwriting. This hand is a miracle of creation, a living embodiment of the intelligence of God. It is alive with the energy of God.

Thus is every part of our body, inside and out. We are a beautiful interplay of interwoven and integrated elements. We are the spirit, intelligence, and love of God put into a fleshly form. We were born into this delightful form; it was generously given to us for our use in this life. It is ours to respect, to feed, to enjoy, and to use carefully. Being physical (with awareness) is prayer, for it is a living expression of the energy of God within us. Inhabiting our body mindfully is sensory prayer.

Sensory prayer is not a matter of thinking about God every time we do something with our senses. It is prayerful enough to be present. If we really believe God to be in our bodies, then when we eat and truly taste, we are praying with our mouths. We needn't say the words "thank you" in order to be expressing gratitude to the Creator. Washing our skin, we pray to the God of skin simply with our wakeful touch. It is enough to just do it with attention. This is because attention brings with it curiosity, reverence, and gratitude. We can't help it. Just to feel the muscles strain as we pull and rake weeds, to willingly give ourselves to the moment, we automatically come upon reverence and gratitude.

However, we do not always live in peaceful harmony with our bodies. We are not always present in our senses. We get sick, we feel anxious, and create tremendous stress, giving ourselves headaches, high blood pressure, and sometimes even killing our body with disharmony. If we even stop for a few minutes to pay attention to our bodies, we will discover little contractions instantly, minute stresses that are physical manifestations of thought and emotion.

But our physical disease, stress, headaches—even our little thought-contractions—are ways in which the divine energy of life and health is attempting to be heard. Through our physical disharmony God is saying "Stop! Pay attention! Something's wrong here! Look at what you're doing! Go another direction, for this one doesn't lead to harmony!" As such, physical problems are red flags, warning messages that are given to us by God's health within us when we stray off the road of health. This information enables us to respond, reflect, pray, and cooperate again with the divine force of health and harmony within our body.

I am not saying that all physical disease is a direct result of our thoughts and emotions, that we create cancer ourselves, for instance. While this may be possible, it is not always so. There is an element of chaos in this universe that cannot be explained away by neat little theories. Bad things do not always happen for a good reason. Part of God's body includes an element of destruction, disharmony, and disease. We may never understand why the world was created "imperfectly" by a perfect creator.

Nevertheless, more often than not we can do something about our physical condition. We can respond to the red flags that our divine source of health raises along the roadside. We can exercise, eat carefully, and watch how our mind and our emotions create mischief in our bodies. God inhabits our body as the source of intelligent harmony; we can cooperate with this resource by paying attention and working with, rather than against it.

In the end, our body will die. Our mind, spirit, soul, whatever you want to call it, will resurrect in some way, just as our physical body will resurrect into nutrition for the earth. In the meantime, our bodies are ours to enjoy: to celebrate God's life within us, to do marvellous things, to make love, even to create more humans. Our bodies can be our teacher, as God rises up within us to warn us about and direct not only our physical well-being, but our spiritual and emotional health as well. Our body, in a very real sense, is God's body.

RELATIONSHIPS

The next widest circle of God's body is that of relationships, especially those which we call family. Family may consist of spouse and children, but it also can include dear friends, long-time companions, parents, or others. Family is not always found in the nuclear model of Western culture. Jesus' natural family was seeking him out in an early phase of his ministry, distraught over his seemingly crazy behavior and words. But he had made other, even deeper bonds by this time. When informed of their search for him, he asked the question "'Who are my mother and my brothers?' And looking at those who sat around him, he said, 'Here are my mother and my brothers! Whoever does the will of God is my brother and sister and mother'" (Mark 3:33–35). So in speaking of "family," whether that is the traditional nuclear model, a committed homosexual couple, a single parent with children, a group of close friends, or any other familial form, God's grace can be seen working through this next circle of God's body, the family.

A significant way in which God works toward wholeness in this familial circle is in the process of emotional growth. It is often here that the fire of intimacy both nurtures and challenges the individuals involved. God's love and judgment are made clear in intimate relationships over time. We come to know forgiveness, unconditional acceptance, the truth about ourselves, and the way forward through death and resurrection.

If God is the force of love and truth in all of creation, then God's body is surely found in this crucible of love and truth we call the family. Many families are not such crucibles, but the potential is there. The choice is always before us: to pay attention to the needs of the other and to be as honest as we can be; or to serve our own self-centered needs and hide from reality. Many grow up in families whose parents, who are responsible for setting the initial direction, choose the latter. How do we make the choice to incarnate God's love and truth in the family?

All of us are self-centered, to one a degree or another. Some of it is natural. As babies, we have to be, and our concerns are basic: food, health, warmth, nurture. But as time goes by our self-centered concerns get more complicated. We want things to work out our way, we want people to behave as we wish, we want to be able to do what we want to do, and we want these things sometimes at the expense of others. These desires are stronger or weaker depending on the individual, but we all have them. We inherit this self-centeredness as soon as we are born into the broken human condition. We are influenced by original sin from the beginning.

In committed relationships, our self-centeredness comes up against the other's self-centeredness, resulting in a collision. We blame one another at first, but with grace we eventually realize that each of us must learn to die to our self-centeredness. At times, the needs of the other and the needs of the family group become more important than one's own individual needs, and once this becomes obvious, we die to ourselves. The small self is crucified. What is resurrected is true love. Love then becomes experienced in our common concern for the family. We are not looking out for ourselves so much as much as we are looking out for the family, in order that it may be a place of mutual concern and support.

What makes possible this shift from self-centeredness to love is the irritating, healing action of the truth. An alcoholic or abusive parent will create suffering for everyone, and the truth will manifest itself, if not in direct words, then through indirect actions. Others will act out angrily, making it impossible to pretend that all is well. Some may leave, throwing the abuser back on himself in truthful suffering and isolation. Eventually, even in more subtle forms of familial self-centeredness, the truth will come out. There is really no hiding place. We can pretend, by shoving the truth and its messengers underground. But it and they will return to haunt us all, and the truth will come out. "Nothing [is] secret that will not become known." (Luke 12:26).

It is the choice of repentance (turning) and the action of God's grace that makes it possible for the truth, however directly or indirectly expressed, to set us free. When we choose to turn toward the truth instead of trying to hide it, we die. When we surrender in this way, God begins to move in ways that we don't have to control, and healing takes place in ways we cannot predict. By turning to the truth in the crucible of the family, we unleash the energy of God to make us whole.

And so love and truth, in the context of committed relationship, can become a source of salvation for those involved. Through a family of people who do their best to live in love and truth, God takes on a body. We see God wherever this takes place. In our marriages, with our children, lovers, parents, friends, and spiritual companions, we have the opportunity to be touched directly by the love and judgment of God. This is why marriage is seen as a sacrament (which I would extend to other forms of intimate relationship as well). Sacraments are "outward and visible signs of inward and spiritual grace." This means that God is enfleshed, made visible, through the ordinary form of intimate relationships. Divine grace pours through this vehicle of God's love and judgment.

COMMUNITY

*P*robably the most familiar way Christians find God present in creation is through community. Our tradition, perhaps more than any other, reminds us again and again of this fact. We call Christian community the Body of Christ, his arms and legs and hands and feet. We see ourselves thereby as a physical, living organism that is the body of God, doing God's work of love and service in this world. While there are other forms of community outside the church that will also be manifestations of God's life for the Christian, the parish is the primary place where one learns to see God enfleshed in a group of people and their life together.

Because the parish (and the wider church by extension) is loaded with this kind of significant meaning, we have high expectations. We think that the parish should be a place of Christ's love; its members should be seekers who are serious about their journey; it should be just as well as an agent for justice; and it should be a place of depth and spiritual integrity.

But what we really encounter in the parish is a microcosm of life, because it is open to the public. Anyone who wants to can come and participate, irregardless of his or her ability to love, pray, serve, or be truthful and healthy. While the parish may carry forth these values, it cannot control whether or not its members actually integrate them. Being a part of Christian community over time is therefore a practice of learning to see God in the ordinariness of life. It is not a special, spiritual place where life is different. In a sometimes frustrating but ultimately healthy way, the parish gives us no escape from the reality of our everyday life.

If living within the parish setting is so ordinary, one may ask: Why bother with it? Why not just live one's life, enjoying the ordinariness of the neighborhood, work, school, and family life? Life is hard enough; why bother adding to it another layer of ordinary difficulties and responsibilities?

There was a documentary done some years ago on Spencer Abbey in Massachusetts, called "Monastery." At one point in the film, a young monk was talking about life in the abbey, describing his daily round of working in the fields, going to meetings, talking through the challenges and conflicts of community life, praying, washing his clothes, and fixing dinner. He said that life in the monastery was just like any other life. The only difference is that in the monastery they put a frame around it. They name it holy and look at it through the lens of God's presence. That's all.

This is what a parish does. We go through the ordinary activities one finds elsewhere: education, budgeting, prayer, administration, counseling, reflecting, and acting upon the needs of our society, doing building maintenance, and going through all the normal crises and joys of individual, family, and community life. And then we put a frame around it. We look at this ordinariness together through the frame of theology, symbols, and liturgy. Looking for God's presence, we peek around the corners of the ordinary. Seeking Christ, we stare through the icon of the everyday. Over the years, we learn the skill of seeing the events and actions of life through the liturgical and theological lens of the gospel. We learn to deal with what life gives us, using the incarnation, the cross and resurrection, and the examples of the saints as tools for dealing with reality. The parish gives us practice in working with these tools, and our lives are transformed by the use of them. This practice happens in a wide variety of ways.

First of all, when you attend a parish over time you will be exposed to all of the tragedies, joys, and transitions of life. The parish community provides a denser concentration of these events than does a life without community. Week after week we discuss, pray about, and hear sermons and announcements regarding things that we would not necessarily encounter otherwise. We watch old people age rapidly after a stroke and we see how their family deals with their fragility. A teenager gets killed by a hit-and-run driver while riding his bike. Twins are born to an overworked but grateful family. A seventy-five-year-old widower falls in love with a fifty-year-old woman, and they get married. Divorce. Adultery. Suicide. fiftieth wedding anniversaries. Adoption. Runaway teenagers. Drugs. AIDS. Alcoholism. Sexual abuse. Miraculous physical healing. Unemployment and poverty. Acts of kindness and tremendous generosity. It's all there in the parish.

Every time I make an announcement about some catastrophe or jubilation in the life of a parishioner, it surprises me when dozens of others who don't even know that person spontaneously gasp or smile. They feel it almost as if it happened to them. And it did happen to them, because they are one body. Every week they pray together and shuffle up to the altar rail to consume together the mystical presence of Christ. Every week they hear names of strangers who are in need of healing in the Prayers of the People, and these names take on meaning. Every week they watch old men struggle to breathe with the help of an oxygen tank and young children bounce around in the pew in front of them. This exposure binds people together and broadens everyone.

This dense microcosm of all of life is surrounded and infused with the language and symbols of the Christian faith. The richness of life and the richness of the faith become inseparable. Gold and white vestments, a gorgeous Bach cantata, and a profusion of lilies all help us see courage and hope in the wrinkles and the limp of an old woman. The starkness of the Lenten altar, ashes on the forehead, and the Litany of Penitence remind us of a young woman whose unexpectedly short life was honored the week before in a funeral. Incarnation, death and resurrection, sin and forgiveness, all of these theological and liturgical themes become real as we see them played out in people's lives in our community; and then we hold it all up in sacrament, story, and symbol again and again.

Within the same hour of worship we hear about homelessness and Jesus' love for the lepers. We pray for the people of Sarajevo and hear in the Gospel that the peacemakers are blessed. Sitting next to us is someone in deep grief and we hear a sermon about death and resurrection. A class discusses the practice of contemplative prayer and we notice the stress and agitation of a burned-out businessman. We listen to teaching about sin and judgment and we hear of the effects of childhood abuse upon a Bible classmate. We celebrate the victory of good over evil in the feast of Michaelmas and we see families recovering from alcoholism. Remembering the gift of the Holy Spirit within us on the great day of Pentecost, we watch those who are lost and alone pull themselves, by the grace of God, through another week.

Theology, biblical stories, liturgy, and the practice of prayer become thoroughly mixed in with life's richness in the parish. This affects us. We become infused with the symbols and the language of faith. We are also surrounded by the depth and breadth, the suffering and the glory of this sacred life. Together, these two intermingled forces of symbol and life can change us over the years. While there is no guarantee of this, at least the potential is there. When suffering strikes our home, we have a context and a practice with which we can endure and redeem it. When our finances improve unexpectedly we may think about what we will do with the extra money in a different way. Our priorities shift. Our way of dealing with conflict changes, fear and anger begin to melt as it begins to dawn on us over time that we really are accepted as we are in the parish. We come out of our isolated, privatized life into the breadth, tragedy, and beauty of society as it is included in the community's arena of concern. We work alongside, and come to know and love, types of people that we would never bother to relate to in the neat compartments of our home and work.

We call this conversion of life. Slowly, over the years, we have the chance to become more God-centered, to see God in a wider circle of life. The people of the community and its life of worship and service gradually challenge us to grow. By this action, God is at work within the parish, as an agent of change for individuals, the community itself, and the wider society on which it has an impact. God's creative energy continues to expand outwards into life.

SOCIETY

The circle of God then moves out to a wider radius when it encompasses all those others in the world whom we may only know through their social condition. God is present in all, but is particularly visible in the struggle to move from suffering to redemption, from death to life. As we work for justice and peace, we participate in God's ever-present cosmic energy of redemption and renewal. We become co-creators, co-healers with God. God uses us to accomplish the work of resurrection and wholeness in the world.

All Christians are called into this circle of God. We live in it anyway, whether we consider this circle to be a part of our faith life or not. Either by our silence or by our active participation, we affect large groups of people whom we will never know personally. Most of us vote, we hold opinions and express them, we support institutions through our donations and investments, we help corporations pursue their economic and ecological practices by buying their products, we encourage injustices to continue because we do not try to put a stop to them, and sometimes we make our voice heard in the public forum or by writing our congressional representatives or by joining forces with a political action group. We are already standing in the circle. So it is a matter of whether or not we will admit that God is in this part of creation.

Many church folk who move with their faith into the wider world beyond their family, neighborhood, and parish begin at the level of charity. This is fine, because the world needs charity. Homeless shelters must be run and food must be given out to the hungry. But our baptismal responsibility does not end there, for there are causes beneath the wounds which we dress in our charity. These causes can and should be attended to as well, so that one day our charity will be unnecessary. Unfortunately, many privileged Christians would rather not change the root causes of suffering. Insisting upon staying at the level of charity then becomes a way of keeping people down where they are.

A vivid example of this comes to mind. In the nineteenth century there were intolerable conditions of worker exploitation in the coal mines of England. Men were not safe, they were underpaid and not given the medical care they needed. Many gave their lives to the mines in which they worked. In one town, it was the regular habit of upstanding middle and upper class women to provide charitable services of food baskets and other band-aids for the poor worker families. Some of these women were married to owners and managers of the mines. An angry worker's demonstration was held (and one of the leaders of the demonstration was an Anglican bishop). They carried a large banner through the better parts of town, and that banner shouted out: "Damn Your Charity, We Want Justice!"

When people of faith begin to move into this arena, it is truly amazing what can happen. They can change history. Look at Martin Luther King and the Christian civil rights activists of the fifties and sixties; Gandhi and his nonviolent Hindu followers; medieval monasteries and convents virtually inventing hospitals and shaping education in the Dark Ages; Archbishop Desmond Tutu and other South African Christians bringing about a peaceful end to the evil of apartheid; pacifist Vietnamese Buddhist monks who helped, through their demonstrations and witness, influence American opinion and bring an end to that war; selfless missionaries around the world today, often the only ones bothering to serve miserable refugees and the poorest of the poor, bringing the world's attention to their plight; courageous martyrs in Latin America "bringing down the mighty from their thrones and lifting up the lowly," as Mary's Magnificat so boldly puts it.

People who are strengthened and given clarity of purpose by faith and community cannot be stopped. God's truth within them becomes a living force, pushing inexorably forward until its goal of justice is won. Those who oppose this force with control and a self-serving evil intent will always lose, no matter how strong they may be at first, no matter how many they may kill. Morality does not have power simply because it is a noble value. It has it because God is the creative, redemptive energy within the fight for justice and peace, a force that is greater than worldly power.

And yet, however optimistic we may be about this power, we are not going to fix the world. When we leave this world, no matter how hard we work, there will be just about the same amount of suffering as when we entered it. If we think we are going to make the world better and this becomes our motivation for acting, we may act out of prideful ambition, in order to see the beneficial effects of our hand at work. Reducing the amount of suffering in the world is not the reason for doing the faith-work of justice and peacemaking. We do this faith-work because we are called to "be perfect [whole, complete, integrated] just as your heavenly Father is perfect" (Matt. 5:48). We do justice and peacemaking because we want to be awake to God's presence in all the circles of our life, not just some. We also do it because we are called to love all the children of God. We do justice and peacemaking because we can't not do it.

But since it is God's energy at work through us, we need not be burdened by the social activism we do. It is not our job to change the world. It is not our job to make sure that we provide an atmosphere of love and peace for all sentient beings. There is already a force of love and peace at work, moving like a wave through history and space. This wave provides far more inspiration, judgment, and motivation than we ever can. We are only riding this wave of love and peace. This gives us a lightness, an ability to laugh at ourselves and not take our zealous passion too seriously.

EARTH

On the wall in my office is a large framed photograph of our planet, taken of course, from space. The earth hangs suspended in empty blackness. She is predominantly blue, with white cloud patterns swirling around her. Visible to the viewer are Saudi Arabia and Africa, vast stretches of brown and green. She is perfectly round, like a large friendly face. There are no visible boundaries, no lines we are so accustomed to seeing on maps. It is all one. When I see it in relation to the infinite black space around it, it looks very small, like a jewel. And yet when I try to imagine the size of a person on it, it seems enormous. The photograph is a *koan*. If I spend enough time before it, something just doesn't make sense. How can this home of ours be so perfect in her complexity, providing everything that is needed for all her living beings for whom she so graciously provides a nest? How is it that this physical globe, just one of so many floating masses of matter in the universe, holds under and upon its surface all of humankind's history and culture? How can this be? She is so gracefully noble, so familiar, and so mysterious: here is a holy icon, the very face of God.

This photograph has been one important factor in a major shift of consciousness that has become available for the people of the earth. We can now make no mistake about our primary identity. While many of us are caught in self-centered dreams of tribalism, nationalism or religious cultism, many more of us now cannot shake the image of ourselves as one unified species on one planet, with one interrelated past, present, and future. We are earthlings all, created to live in harmony with all other species of the world: plants, fish, ocean, dirt, insects, and wind. We are all children of the one God, sharing an incredibly beautiful garden in which to suffer, play, and love.

The widest circle of all in our faith expression is when we give our attention to the circle which hangs in my office: the earth. This is where our awareness of God's body moves out into this whole planet and the universe beyond. Here our boundaries of the self really stretch outward to include lizards, whales, spiders, roses, raccoons, banana trees, coyotes, tumbling rivers, shimmering lakes, deserts, bayous, giant redwoods, rocks, mud, ferns, salmon, clouds, rain, snow, tigers, palm trees, burros, snakes, rolling seas, stars, and the vast, black expanse of space.

We are one of the species of the earth, having evolved through its mineral, plant, and animal life. We are a part of the earth and the earth is a part of us. Our actions and even our very breath are effected by and effect, in turn, everything else. The God who made us as we are also made an integrated whole of which we are but only a part. To live in this awareness is to move out of our self-centered, anthropocentric limitations.

To see the animals of the earth as our brothers and sisters, and to view the plants and water of the earth as our soulmates in God is to live in an animated, God-filled world.

What does the Judeo-Christian tradition say about our relationship to the rest of the earth? The Western world has often been held responsible, and rightly so, for the pollution of the world. We, until recently, have been more industrialized and consumptive than the rest of the world. Other societies are seen as living more harmoniously with the land and the sky, because of their ecologically superior spiritual roots. Therefore, Judeo-Christian religious tradition has been blamed for much of the Western world's abuse of the rest of creation. But this is too simplistic a reading of both the societies of the world and the Judeo-Christian tradition. It may be more accurate to say that people around the world often behave in a greedy and short-sighted manner, that industrialized societies around the world have been especially exploitative of their environment, and that Western society has found its justification for this behavior in a misreading of its own religious tradition.

Wherever there is urban industrialization (including, now, in Eastern, third-world, and indigenous people's environments), there is abuse of creation. And so it is not fair to dismiss the Judeo-Christian tradition as a singularly unenlightened spiritual foundation which produces in its followers an incompatible relationship with creation. We just got around to ecological destruction first, being the first urban industrialized nations.

In fact, there is much to be found within the Judeo-Christian tradition which supports an ecologically sensitive life, even if the Western world has at times misread and ignored its spiritual roots while becoming industrialized. Like other religions, the Judeo-Christian tradition began in an agricultural society. Religions that begin in this setting are always, as a matter of survival, grounded in the known integration of individuality, society, God, and earth. A fresh reading of scripture's teaching about creation will assist us in moving back to a healthier point of view that began on the other side of our industrialization.

The first chapter of the first book of the Bible begins with our relationship to the rest of creation. "Then God said, 'Let us make humankind in our image, after our likeness, and let them have dominion over the fish of the sea, and over the birds of the air, and over the cattle, and over all the earth, and over every creeping thing that creeps upon the earth'" (Gen.1:26). Since industrialization, this passage has often been taken as God's carte blanche given to us to use and abuse the world for our selfish purposes. But we must understand this crucial word "dominion."

This word has the same root as "domain." We are given responsibility over (and not the freedom to exploit) God's domain. Here is a basic understanding that God is the master of creation and humankind is not. Men and women are a part of creation that is, all of it, under subjection to and dependent upon God. But because we have been given self-consciousness, we have a special responsibility to carry out. We are God's stewards for the rest of creation. We are given temporary charge over something that is quite clearly not our own. Clearly the biblical charge is to care for God's creation. Stewards are those who are held responsible to care for another's property, and who are accountable for their actions.

There is no Hebrew word for "nature." The pre-industrial Jewish people were less dualistic than we have become; we talk about going outside into nature, as if we could ever leave it. For the Hebrews, all of creation, including people, is one integrated whole. Furthermore, according to the Jews, all of creation is animated with an awareness of God. Jesus, upon his entry into Jerusalem, was criticized for allowing people to praise him. He responded "I tell you, if these were silent, even the stones would shout out" (Luke 19:40). Many of the Psalms are truly panentheistic songs of creation. In Psalm 148, all of creation is called upon to sing praises to their God: sun, moon, stars, sea monsters, fire and hail, snow and frost, stormy wind, mountains, fruit trees and cedars, wild animals and cattle, creeping things and flying birds, and finally people. How could they sing their praises without consciousness, without God's presence within them? I do not think that this is just a metaphor. I really think that God inhabits and gives spiritual awareness to all matter, all creation.

It is this panentheism which gives rise to an expanded understanding of the incarnation. We say that God took on flesh in Jesus, but God also takes on flesh in all of creation. The sacramental churches recognize this broad incarnation through the celebration of rites which hold out the holiness of bread, wine, water, and oil. In addition to these elements, we also bless animals, crosses, houses, icons, boats, candles, vestments, and people. The ordinary stuff of creation is seen as being sacred. How can bread or water be sacred unless God is in it? How can we, therefore, limit our view of God's incarnation to Jesus? All of creation is an incarnation of God.

It is through the rich biblical and theological tradition of our faith that Christians can come to a new relationship with the rest of creation. Through other paths both modern and ancient we are reminded that this world has indeed been made as one living organism of which we are an integral part. Its being is the intelligence and life directed energy of God. It is constantly in motion, dying and being resurrected in impermanence.

A harmonious relationship with the rest of creation begins with prayer, which brings us full circle, back to our interior experience with God. To be responsible stewards we must first be prayerfully awake to the sacredness of the domain over which we have been given charge. In prayer we slow down and begin to look around and within us. We listen, smell, and touch with awareness. When we are awake, we see that the ordinary stuff of each moment contains all that is needed for a holy life. The grass under our bare feet sings praises to God along with us. The water we drink contains life itself. The beggar on the street embodies God. The warmth of the sun brings God's light into our souls. Awakening to this moment, God is released for us into life, and expands outward into our bodies, our relationships, community, society, and the whole created universe in which we live.

Epilogue

Christian faith and practice is a broad path, as broad as life itself. It concerns itself with holiness, our relationships with one another and the earth, awareness, suffering, celebration, sin, guilt, contemplation, seasonal cycles, joy, peace of mind, love, surrender, effort, community, servanthood, forgiveness, justice, identity, death, and eternal life.

Christianity is for those who need a path that affirms and uses the ordinary of this world. It is for those who sense that Jesus' path is the way that leads to life. But in order for the Christian form to have any impact upon us and the world in which we live, we must bring its rich themes and transcendent wisdom into our real life experience. The themes of this book are the ways I know in which we can do this.

The responsibility for building this vision of a healthy, worldly, and mature faith lies with each of the members of the church. The clergy and lay leaders certainly carry a lion's share of this responsibility. But as individual seekers in the church look for a mature and open church community to support their own faith life, they need to realize that they must help to create the very thing they seek. This is part of our spiritual practice. And so if we want the church to be an open, experience-based form that leads us back into life, we must work to make it so. We must all be transformers of the church.

The church exists to celebrate and serve the creative energy and purpose of God. Ultimately, if (and only if) the church is really needed in the world to bring people to God, a transformation of the church will indeed take place. For God will rise up through our cultural circumstances, our historical development as a species, our efforts and awareness as individuals, and create new life for the world through the Christian form. In the end, it is God who will set the gospel free.

An Instruction for Practicing Contemplative Prayer

WHAT IS CONTEMPLATIVE PRAYER?

There are many ways of praying and meditating. At any given time, one way will be more helpful than others for each of us. The form of contemplative prayer I describe herein is only one method, and it is not for everybody. It has, however, made a significant difference in my spiritual life. It has brought me into reality and into the transformative power of God's grace more fully than any other form of prayer I have found. I have adapted this method of contemplative prayer from Zen meditation as taught by Joko Beck of the Zen Center of San Diego (see her books, *Everyday Zen*, Harper and Row, and *Nothing Special*, HarperSanFrancisco).

Most forms of contemplative prayer and meditation begin with the assumption that we are trying to get to a mental/ physical state of open, empty, non-distracted sensory awareness;

we may call this a state of being "centered in God." In order to reach this goal, concentration upon some image or thought is often used to bring one back to the purpose at hand once we discover that we are distracted. In this sense we are using concentration to try to stay in the desired state.

The contemplative prayer I know has a different goal. We are not trying to get anywhere. We are simply doing the best we can to become aware of what is going on in our thoughts, our bodies, and in the world around us. In order to do this, instead of concentrating on something, we just watch what is already there. If we are thinking about something, we notice what we are thinking, and we also notice the bodily sensations that go along with those particular thoughts. We do not try to "let go" of thoughts, emotions, or sensations, and we do not try to make them go away. We simply notice and name them and feel what is there. If we are upset, we feel the distress. If we are worried, we feel the fear. If we happen to be enjoying an awareness of our breath, or the sounds around us, or the air on our skin, then we just experience that sensation. Whatever is going on is what is going on, and being present to it by noticing and naming it is being present. Being aware through our senses, without thought, is not the only way to be "really present." We can also be really present in the moment by watching, feeling, and naming our so-called distractions (which usually take up the bulk of our time).

By simply watching, feeling, and naming, we begin to see some interesting things if we stick with it long enough. Thoughts, emotions, and bodily sensations fall into patterns. Much of what we see is painful for us to admit. We begin to learn that we worry all the time, or we plan constantly, or we are forever escaping into fantasy, or we are criticizing ourselves or others, or trying to figure everything out. We learn the things we habitually do in our minds in the vain attempt to control reality. Trying to control reality is the heart of our separation from

God, since it attempts to put ourselves in God's place, saying *my* will, not thine be done; it keeps us from seeing life clearly, since the ego is desperately trying to interpret life to our advantage; it is what motivates our manipulative and non-loving behavior toward others as we attempt to make things go our way. Therefore getting to know the specific ways in which we try to control reality becomes extremely important.

These habitual patterns of thought and emotion (that effect our behavior all day long) are most directly discovered as we sit in silence and watch our "distractions." For our "distractions" are the ways in which we try to control the threatening, out of control experience of just sitting in silence! Our little minds go wild trying to jockey for position, throwing all sorts of situations up on the screen so that we can practice our usual methods of control. The mind brings up problems and worries so that our patterns of control can kick in and go to work. As we watch this process taking place, we come to know the specific ways in which we try to assert the illusory control of the ego. As we come to know these patterns, we get to the heart of our separation from God and life; we get to the basic habitual sins that keep us from loving and serving others with an open and accepting heart.

The way in which this becomes prayer is through the general awareness that God is *in* our thoughts, bodies, emotions, senses, and even our "distracting" worries and plans. God is in us in every way. If this is so, then when we are present to what is, we are present to God in our life. To awaken to awareness of whatever is happening is to come awake within and before God. Furthermore, to watch and admit where we really are in our separation and sin (rather than trying to be in an ideal "spiritual" state) is the most honest form of vulnerability before God that I know.

Something graceful happens when we are this vulnerable and honest. Holding ourselves as we are before God slowly leads us out of the fears, ambitions, anxiety, and other ways in which we try to control life. When we offer our separative patterns in prayer, God helps us see their self-centered, illusory, and useless nature. In some measure they then lose their grip over us and we are freed from them. What is left is a greater degree of loving availability—a clear and willing ability to be present to the world—to life as it is, and to others. This is our true nature, the nature of God. The wonderful thing is that we don't have to (and can't, in fact) change ourselves in order to accomplish this nature. All we have to do is, as honestly as we can, hold ourselves as we are before God. God will do the rest.

When we sit in contemplation, we begin with a bow and an opening prayer that we may be given grace to pay attention and see ourselves as we truly are. We then sit in silence and begin to watch. In the back of our minds we know that we sit in the presence of God, who sees, accepts, and loves even what we cannot see, accept, or love. When our time ends, we bow and pray again in gratitude, with the acknowledgment that God will take what has been offered and transform us to become the people we have been created to be.

PLACE, POSTURE, AND TIME

Contemplation can be done anywhere: on the bus, at one's desk, outdoors on the patio. But it is helpful for me to have a daily, regular, uninterrupted time and an area in my house that is dedicated for this purpose. I have a wooden box on which I place a candle, a small icon of Jesus, perhaps a flower, and incense. The purpose of this area is not to create a little world which we can enjoy during contemplation, into which we can escape. It is to set the tone. Having a place, a little altar in my house, it is easier for me to begin the daily habit of contemplation when I sit down there. This area should be simple, not too precious, and should probably change in makeup and even location every once in awhile so we don't get too attached to it. It should be against the wall and either low or high enough so that when we sit, our eyes fall on a blank surface.

Your posture needs to be straight when sitting, in order to stay alert and to avoid sore muscles. Slouching, while it may feel comfortable for a few minutes, creates tension and tiredness in the muscles. Sitting up with a straight spine is the most natural and restful position for your back over time. This posture is accomplished by using a meditation pillow (zafu), a kneeling bench, or a firm chair. When using a zafu or a kneeling bench, the floor should be covered by a soft rug or cushioned by a mat such as a zabuton, made especially for meditation. This is so your legs and knees don't wear out.

When using a zafu, sit on the cushion in either a full or half-lotus position. The cushion can be wedged forward slightly with another small pillow to ensure that when sitting, the hips will be pitched forward slightly as well. A kneeling bench consists of two upright supports, five to eight inches in height, with a seat that is approximately six inches deep and twelve inches wide, and slanted downwards toward the front so that again, the hips pitch forward a bit. Kneel on the floor, placing the feet and shins under the bench, and then sit on the seat of the bench. A kneeling bench can be made easily by someone with a few woodworking skills, but you'll have to test the angle and dimensions first by setting up a board and some kind of supports. A chair can be used if it is firm. Sit either with a firm pillow against the small of your back, or on the front half of the chair so that your back is not resting against the back of the chair.

Thus situated on pillows, bench, or chair, place the hands in your lap, one set of fingers resting on top of the others, the tips of your thumbs touching each other. This is to create a circular sense of connectedness in the body. It will look as if you are holding a large, invisible egg. Imagine that a thread is attached to the back of the top of your head and that it is gently pulling upwards. The effect is that your chin drops down a bit, your spine is lengthened, and there is a small arch in the bottom of your back. Your chest opens up by placing your shoulders back a little. This should be an erect but not rigid position. You should be physically alert and and also relaxed.

Should you be physically unable to accomplish what I have described, find some position that enables your body to be both alert and restful. It is important to be in a position which enables wakeful, relaxed attention for a half hour or more. There is nothing holy about body position. It is a question of what works.

If you are new to this form of meditation, begin with fifteen minutes. You may wish to stretch the time spent in prayer to a half hour or forty-five minutes as you get accustomed to it. I use a timer on my electronic watch. Its beep is unobtrusive but noticeable. When I use a timer, I'm not thinking about how long it's been, whether I can stop soon. I'm just obedient to the beep.

THE BODY

*L*ooking straight ahead and down at an angle of forty-five degrees, the eyes remain half open. Fix your gaze upon a spot and keep it there. Start paying attention to your breath. Do not change it. Just notice what it is like. Follow it as it goes in and out. Feel the inrush of air as it passes through the nostrils and follow it down through the throat and into the lungs. As the lungs contract, follow the breath back out. Follow it over and over. Sounds will occur, your nose will itch, muscles will feel temporarily sore. Without acting on any of these physical sensations, just notice them. Sit through them, even if they are distressing, and let them be what they are. We should be still, because even the smallest motions to relieve discomfort are a way of escaping where we are. They are a form of entertainment, a way of avoiding reality. Our eyes, even our tongue should remain motionless.

If your sitting position is correct there will be no damage done by enduring some physical pain when it comes. In fact, this helps our resolve to be present through everything. On the other hand, some stubbornly sit, incorrectly and in pain, for long periods and do real harm. There is no point to this kind of macho attitude. If you need assistance from someone more experienced in sitting meditation, seek it out. If you must shift positions to correct yourself, do so. Eventually, however, a position that works should be found that does not require even the slightest adjustment during sitting. We should sit still, through all physical, mental, and emotional protests that inevitably come up with.

The first time I learned how to accept and move through physical distress was when I was a swimmer in high school. On cold mornings we would line up on the cement wearing only a racing suit. Covered with goose bumps, I'd shiver uncontrollably as the coach spoke to us. One day I realized that my body was just cold. It was just coldness. I could feel the coldness without adding emotional distress to the physical sensation. Coldness was just, well, cold.

PAYING ATTENTION

*B*eginning with attention to the breath and continuing to sit, our mind then begins to play its games. It will think about whatever it wants to think about, and our body will respond with little contractions; we can't control this. We shouldn't think about what comes up or analyze it. We just name it: "worrying about getting that project done" or "thinking about my sister." Keep it simple and very specific. Don't take it any further ("thinking about my sister and wondering why she said that. . . . I'll bet what she really meant was . . ."). There is a

place for analysis of our thoughts and feelings but contemplation is not that place. By simply naming the thought we un-
hook ourselves from it. It just becomes a passing occurrence
which we observe, and then watch as it fades away.

We then experience our thought or feeling physically. By
paying attention to the physical sensations that accompany
thoughts and emotions, we go to the core. We cut through the
layers of fantasy, analysis, interpretation, and distress which we
layer on top of thoughts and feelings. We don't judge or worry
about what is going on. We simply let it be the specific physical
sensation which, at the root of it, it is. Thinking something is a
"bad emotion," for instance, can then give way to an active curiosity: What, exactly, is the body doing right now as a result of
this thought or emotion? Worry or controlling thoughts then
become a specific sensation in the body: just *this*, whatever it is.

Sometimes in order to sensitize ourselves to our bodily
sensations and reactions, we must study ourselves. Some people
have a difficult time in feeling their bodies at all, or can only
feel very obvious things. If this is the case, spend the first ten
minutes of each time in contemplation, or even a whole half
hour, in doing a body-check. Slowly work from one part of your
body to another. Really try to feel the soles of your feet, the middle of your back, your scalp, your tongue. A very good guide to
this kind of work is Jon Kabat-Zinn's *Full Catastrophe Living,*
which came out of his work with people in chronic pain.

Here's an example of what happens when we pay attention to thoughts, feelings, and bodily sensations. Let's say that
every time I contemplate, I find myself thinking about a con-
flicted relationship of which I am afraid. I may even feel hatred
toward the person, imagining that they are the cause of my
problems. When I realize I am doing this, I name it: thinking of
a friend, fear, anger, imagining a disaster, whatever it is. I then
pay close attention to and name the physical sensations created
by the thought–emotion. Tight stomach, fluttery chest, light

head, sweat on the brow, clammy palms. I let these sensations be there and watch them. I hold them before God, accepting them and acknowledging that right now, this is where I am.

Or I may find myself spinning out a fantasy of success. I get ideas for the building project we're working on at church. These ideas lead me into an imagined outcome. People are smiling and they like me. I am somebody. Someday they will remember me with affection after I die. I even hear their respectful conversations about me after my death. I enjoy listening in. When I become aware that I am doing this, I name it: imagining success, desire for attention. I notice the physical sensations. Increased heartbeat, shortened breath, eyes open wide. I hold this before God in honest awareness, just *this*, accepting my patterns of behavior honestly.

One hundred thoughts in a half hour all seem to be different, but underneath their individual forms they may all come from the same place. We may have a regular pattern of generating thoughts out of fear that something terrible will happen in the future or that people won't like us. Thousands of variations on this theme are possible. We may have a pattern of generating thoughts out of the desire to get things done and done well, in order to get what we want as soon as possible, and this pattern manifests itself endlessly.

I knew a man who used to label these deep-level thought patterns with numbers. When we talked about it he said that currently, for him, #1 was imagining conflict, #2 was sexual fantasies, #3 was ambition, and #4 was random thoughts. After observing his mind over years, he was able to see these familiar patterns underneath specific thoughts. As a thought or emotion arose in the moment, he would look at it, categorize it by number (oh, another #3!) and watch it fade away.

And so we name the thought or emotion at hand, feel the bodily sensation, and then drop below the surface and ask ourselves, if it isn't already obvious, "What is driving this thought or emotion?" A worried fixation about getting something done at work later that day leads us more deeply into an awareness of our fear of looking bad. A thought about a conversation yesterday leads us to the same place. So does thinking about the clothes we'll wear to meet a certain person. And so on. After awhile, our basic motivating patterns become pretty obvious.

It may even be that all of us are driven by only two basic patterns: attachment and aversion. Attachment is the clinging to what we want and aversion is the fear of what we don't want. Averse to pain, we drink heavily. Averse to loneliness, we use others. Averse to suffering, we ignore the cries of the poor. Averse even to ourselves, we rush from activity to activity. Attached to pleasure, we grasp after one ultimately unsatisfying experience after another. Attached to feeling the rush of newness, we spend too often and too much. Attached to fantasies about our life, we miss the moment. Attached to getting what we want, we manipulate people.

Attachment and aversion are the two poles of Buddhist *samsara* (the endless cycle of suffering). Attachment and aversion also separate us from God. As such, they are the root of all sin and suffering. In our drivenness toward our attachments and away from our aversions, we lose sight of life, of God. We become blinded by these illusions, these idols. These basic motivating forces lead us to neurotic, obsessive, and sometimes destructive behavior.

WHAT GOOD IS IT?

Over time, the patterns which we learned at a very early age begin to lose their power over us. With the help of God, we begin to recognize that they are just imaginary solutions to life's problems, for they don't work. Instead, they re-create suffering in our own lives and the lives of others. Over time, with awareness, our patterns of trying to control reality begin to melt away. They lose their power over us, and we play these games a little less. What then replaces the ego-game of control is a still, clear, compassionate availability to life and to other people. What is left after our fearful separate patterns begin to melt is the pure joy of simply being alive.

Practicing this daily in contemplation for a concentrated half hour a day makes it that much easier to do in the moment for the rest of the day, right in the midst of activity. After all, this is the goal of contemplative practice, that one may learn to practice it all the time. During a meeting, when we find ourselves tightening up, we do a quick check of thoughts, emotions, or bodily reactions, or discover a pattern of attachment or aversion beneath that is very familiar. Acknowledging it and offering it to God, we become freer to be present without the extra layer of separation/sin. We move out of our prison of destructive and self-centered patterns into an empty, still, and clear point of appreciative awareness and availability. These moments of clarity, just like in contemplation, grow from fleeting glimpses to regular and longer periods, in all sorts of circumstances.

This practice makes it more possible for us to enjoy life and to be clear in our actions. Less caught up in our reactions, we can be with what is. Less blinded by ourselves, we see what is in front of us. Mowing the lawn, we dance with the roar of the mower and the smell of fresh cut grass. Having lunch with a friend, we taste the food and appreciate the other's face, her voice, his concerns. Fixing a clogged toilet, we experience, without judgment, sloshing in the messiness and we enjoy the energy of problem solving. Listening to frustrated voices at a long meeting, we move through our reactions and see them with truth and compassion. We say yes to all of life. And since life is immersed in God, we are herein saying yes to God.

In this awareness of what is, we are awake and fully alive. We feel our breath going in and out. We feel our skin and the air around it. We appreciate the person in front of us as a child of God. Sounds of chirping birds in the garden, traffic going by, voices in adjacent yards are all a magnificent soundscape. Even conflict has a kind of amazing and interesting energy that we can appreciate. It all washes through us. We feel like a mountain. We are empty of self and full of life's essence, of God. This stillness may not come at all on any given day. When it does, it may last for only five seconds, but it is a glimpse of heaven.

The practice of contemplation is one way to awaken to the beauty and pain of life as it is. The God of all being is found in all, and the more we awaken to life, the more we awaken to God.